Published in 2005 by Drink Australia Pty Limited

Drink Australia Pty Ltd.
PO Box 873
Newtown, 2042
NSW Australia

A CIP catalogue record for this publication is available from the National Library of Australia.

ISBN 0-9752123-9-7

Author: Hayden Wood
Designer/Photographer: Esmeralda Wood
Editor: Sunil Badami
Pre-Press by George Maniatis - Spinninghead
Printed by 1010 Printing International Limited.
Printed in China. Printed 2005.

Those who may be susceptible to reactions from raw egg, nuts including peanut oil should be mindful of some of the products used in these recipes.

It's the host's responsibility to provide an environment where guests can enjoy alcohol in moderation, accompanied by food. Where possible, drink one glass of water to every cocktail and make sure you get home safely by organising taxi transport.

www.theliquidkitchen.com
www.mondobartender.com

woody's liquid kitchen

hayden wood

for amalia and jaime

contents

happy times, good friends, hip drinks

When it comes time to break out the cocktail glasses and shake up a storm, there's usually something to be celebrated. But now it seems the good old cocktail has made its mark on the culture, enjoying a renaissance that seems to keep on going. After having a few good cocktails in one of the many new and groovy cocktail bars that have sprung up lately, pretty much everyone is giving it a bash for any reason…no special occasion, just having a cocktail.

I've met a lot of people on my travels who loved the first two books, and have begun regularly mixing their drinks at home. And more and more have told me how they regard their cocktail shaker, blender and juicer as important as any of their other kitchen equipment. I've realised that a need has sprung up for some decent cocktail-mixing equipment, and that's what's been keeping me busy over the last year: developing my own line of groovy cocktail equipment to keep you guys mixing…oh, and then there's this book.

Putting pen to paper, I suddenly realised that the more I taught people about mixing drinks in their own liquid kitchen, the more I learnt. Meeting the people who read and mixed from the books, finding out what they did, and what worked in their own recipes, was exhilarating - and educational! It's been great to share some of their drink recipes, and more importantly, their stories. You can also see more hip drinks from more of my shakin' friends at www.theliquidkitchen.com

You don't need to be an expert - or an alcoholic! - to mix great tasting and interesting drinks for yourself, your friends and loved ones. All you'll need is a kitchen, some basic tools, a few simple techniques and some inspired drinks recipes from around the world, and soon you'll be making any occasion a special one!

And all you need to get started is in these pages!

Go on, get up, get going and get mixing!
Shake it up baby!

can you shake it?

can you shake it?

Being a liquid kitchen mix maniac is not as complex as it sounds. As you look through the book you'll notice that there are some drinks that take more time to prepare than others. Try starting on the easy drinks, and get comfortable with the whole process. Practice makes perfect. And the best part with practising cocktails is you get to drink your mistakes away!

The next step is allocating a little time for preparation before your party or drinks session commences. Cooking up a glaze or preparing some flavoured sugar are some of the little things that are dead easy to do - and often overlooked - but paying attention to the little things can make you look like a cocktail genius when a session gets started. And saves a whole lot of waiting when things get shakin'.

A great way to keep the night rocking is to delegate. Ask your friends to help make drinks with you. Give someone a shot at making the fruit ice or fruit skewers. Seal the cocktail shaker together and pass it around so everyone can have a good shake. Team participation makes for bundles of laughs, keeps everyone occupied and takes the pressure off you, so you can enjoy your night... and your company.

Organising a cocktail party always starts with the menu: the drinks you'd like to make. From there, make up a list of ingredients, and note how many of the drinks share common ingredients. Obviously, the more common ingredients you have, the less you'll have to organise - but aim for a diverse and varied list to keep everyone happy and topped-up. And a good host will always include something non-alcoholic to ensure that the designated driver isn't left out.

Jotting down a few ideas and looking through recipes, think of the food everyone would like to eat, then work out which drinks you'd like to mix. Then you're all set to get shakin'.

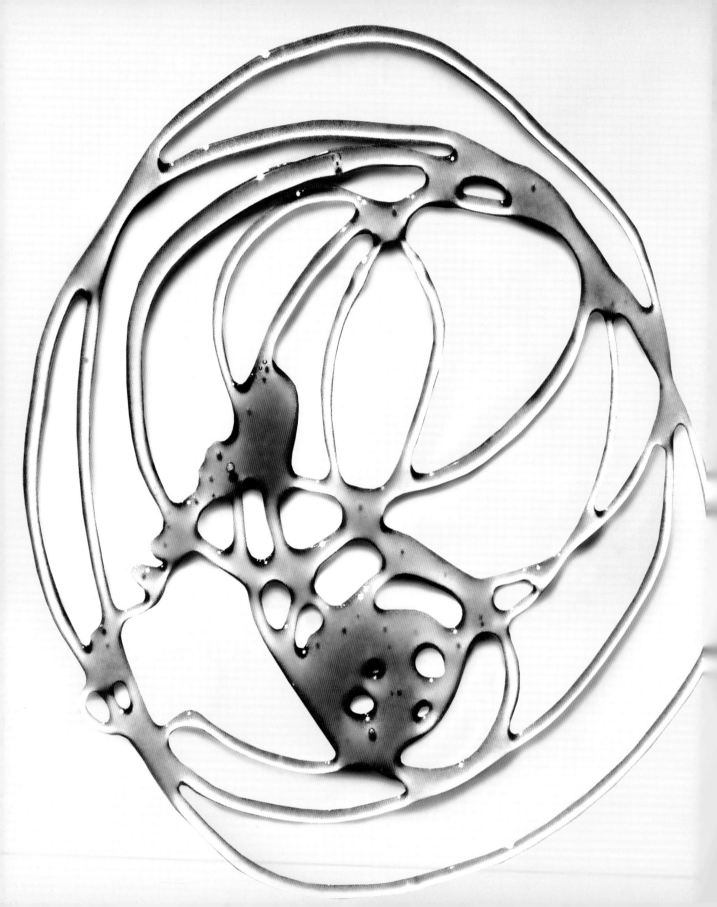

methods and hip things

These are the accessories to all the recipes in the book. They're the bells and whistles that add magic to any drink, no matter how simple. Again, it's the little things that make all the difference. As Esmeralda says, you can get away with wearing anything, as long as your nails and hair are done. Life's too short for boring drinks.

My first book, Groovy Drinks, explored concentrated mixers flavoured with such ingredients as caramelised apple and cinnamon; pear and ginger; or lychee and lemongrass, adding intriguing twists to classic cocktails.

My second book, Party Drinks, drew on sugar syrups and their variations like summer pear, candy apple and ginger flavoured syrups for great party cocktails that were easy to make and even easier to drink.

But one of the most interesting and exciting ingredients in this book are Glazes. These are inspired by my wonderful old mentor Pierre Vuilleumier, a very Gallic and very talented chef who took me on as a waiter many years ago. Some of his desserts included Glazes and recently mum sent me a jar of his wonderful Orange Glaze. Pierre's products are so good they're now for sale everywhere in New Zealand under the Esk label.

So the glaze used on a cake or dessert can be used to flavour cocktails and the effect is lavish! I like them because they are more concentrated than syrups and thus take up less room in the fridge and at the mixing station. The alcohol many contain gives them a greater shelf life.

So adorn your drinks. People drink with their eyes before their mouth and when they finally get to taste it, the extra time you've spent in the kitchen will be met with praise and no doubt rewarded with kitchen karma love.

party blueprint

When people tell me about their cocktail parties, they always seem to start off nicely. But somehow they end up like a runaway truck… everyone loses the plot, drinks that get made end up not being drunk, and those who can remember the end of the night would prefer to forget it.

It certainly doesn't take a genius to work out that if it's hard work for the host, chances are they won't be having another party any time soon. To prevent yet another truck crash - or worse, yet another boring spell of cheap wine and local beer, here are a few good ideas to ensure you're always the quintessentially chilled hip cocktail host.

I call it a party blueprint because if you follow it every time, you can be sure of building a great atmosphere at any party.

organisation

Getting a good foundation down ensures that everything runs smoothly during the night. Setting up a drinks station so that someone can add garnishes or chop ingredients at one end while someone else is mixing drinks, means nobody will be left out - or worse, left without a drink! Ensuring that garnishes are prepared beforehand, that ingredients are readily at hand and having a clear idea of what you want to make ahead of time will actually free you up for a little more experimentation and a lot more fun on the night.

responsibility

Having your own style of hospitality is what attracts people back to your place to enjoy your company. Being generous doesn't necessarily mean giving more than your guests can cope with. Pay attention to the little details and anticipate their needs by offering water or non-alcoholic alternatives and good food with your mixed drinks. Framing the limits will help keep your friends looking good and ensure everyone can play as hard as they like, within the limits you've set.

If you have a guest that'll put everything in a drink,
including the kitchen sink... it could be time to pull the plug.

kitchen set up

imagination

Styling drinks, like your wardrobe or interior decoration, is all about personal taste. Recipes are just a guide to get your own creative juices flowing, so be creative and try your own.

confidence

If you've had a crack at drink mixing before, chances are you would've learnt quite a bit on your first go, so hand that knowledge on to those who've never tried it before. Building on your and your friends' knowledge of mixed drinks will add to your confidence. Not just in yourself, but in giving your friends the confidence to not only try a drink, but get in the kitchen and mix one up.

So, essentially all you'll need to get your gathering of friends mixing drinks is two parts organisation, one part responsibility, a dash of imagination and a little confidence.

stock

Take note of the following basic bits that'll keep you in good form when you have the next 'little' gathering. If you have just two of each of these things in each category you'll be able to mix a good variety of drinks.

alcohol	vodka, gin, rum, tequila, liqueurs, bitters and champagne
mixers	juices, nectar, syrups, glazes, dairy, still and sparkling water
dry	napkins, straws, spices, sugar and herbs and spices
fresh	fruit, herbs, plenty of ice
tools	cocktail shaker, mixing glass, hawthorne strainer, jugs and bowels, pour spouts that fit bottles to allow a calculated pour, blender, rind or zest cutter, muddling pin, a few good pots and a few empty bottles, a good ice bucket, a couple of tea towels
glassware	martini, highball, old-fashioned, cocktail, wine, shot glasses, cups and bowls

space

Working with the space you have is half the fun. I started with nothing more than a 50cm square fridge top in a tiny shoe box apartment. Thankfully I've expanded a little, which, in comparison, is quite luxurious. However, if pushed, I'm sure I could still mix it up with the best of them on top of a bar fridge!

Every cocktail bar and cocktail maker has a mixing station, where all the necessary tools and ingredients can be laid out, almost like an assembly line, so that the work flows in easy steps and there's some method to the madness. You can do this working from the sink in the kitchen, but even if you set up a table outside the kitchen - in the lounge room or the garden, keeping the mixing station 'assembly line' in mind will keep you cool and the drinks mixed quick.

Here are a few pointers to help:
Keep fruit to the end of the mixing station to allow easy and quick selection and preparation. Keeping it to the end means someone can be getting ingredients together while another finishes mixing in the middle of the mixing station.

Keep the glassware and ice bucket a safe distance from the mixing action. Glass is your friend but it can also be your enemy. A chipped piece of glass in the ice is impossible to pick out and can mean a whole lot of ice - or worse, a drink! - is wasted. So be sure to use a proper metal ice scoop and not a glass when scooping ice.

Although you can't move your kitchen sink, it does have some bearing on the placement of such things as the cocktail shakers and the rubbish bin. If the shakers are going to be washed all the time, they should be kept close to the tap. As the sink is the main drainage point of the operation, overs in the bottom of glasses, the 'slops', can be tossed into a sieve or colander in the sink. Of course, once that fills up, the remains of the slops will need to be discarded so it's ideal to keep a rubbish bin handy to the sink.

Watch out for spills on the floor. Keep a mop or old towel handy to soak up the occasional floor cocktail.

sugar

sugar

Throughout this book, you'll note the use of sugar in a lot of recipes. Sugar is to drink mixing what salt is to cooking. It enhances flavours and often disguises the hot alcohol flavour in many cocktails. It's also a pretty good natural preservative.

The sweet things in life can lure almost everyone back for more...
who's your sugar daddy?

I've always loved the way caster sugar dissolves so quickly and effectively in cold drinks. However, there's a wide variety of sugars that can add an exotically subtle finish. Try any of these sugars in place of standard white or caster sugar for an intriguing twist to any recipe.

regular sugar

fine granulated sugar = table sugar = standard granulated sugar = extra-fine granulated sugar, the standard table sugar with which everyone's familiar.

superfine sugar

caster sugar = ultra fine sugar = bar sugar = instant dissolving sugar = caster sugar. This dissolves more quickly, and is recommended for sweetening drinks, syrups, concentrated mixers and glazes.

daddy

brown sugar

It's not just a great Stones track! Its caramel flavour, soft mooshy texture and dark brown colour makes it a very popular alternative to standard white sugar. Available in almost every supermarket, it's less refined with a more creamy, natural sweetness.

palm sugar (also known as coconut sugar or java sugar)

You can find palm sugar in Indian or Asian markets. Made from the sap of date or coconut palm trees, it's much more flavoursome than granulated sugar. It's often sold in solid cakes, wrapped in paper, and should crumble readily when squeezed. Matching palm sugar with fresh vivacious flavours like lime and mint in the Mojito on page 343, is a good way to start experimenting with different sugars.

coarse sugar

This has larger grains than regular granulated sugar. It's slow to change colour or break down at high temperatures. If size matters and you like large crystals in your sugar bowl, coarse sugar will give you more visual character than added flavour. Also good for rimming glasses (see page 25).

sugar syrup

Makes 700ml / 33½oz (1 bottle) or approximately 23 drinks
350g / 11½oz white sugar
350ml / 11½oz water

Stir ingredients in pot over medium heat for 5 minutes or until sugar has dissolved, then pour into a sterilized bottle . Keep sealed in fridge for up to two weeks.

sugar substitutes

reduce

Up to ⅓ of the sugar in most recipes can be eliminated without replacement. This will reduce calories in a recipe, but the flavour will be less sweet; glazes will be paler, and sometimes a little more tart or dry in flavour; drinks will seem stronger in alcohol, as sugar disguises the hot alcohol sensation in your mouth. This may prompt you to lower the alcohol quantity in your recipe.

Remember the saying,..A spoon full of sugar helps the medicine go down? it's also the most delightful ingredient that makes the majority of your cocktails taste rich and full of flavour.

honey

Substitute ¾ of the sugar or half the sugar syrup for honey. If replacing the sugar syrup, increase the amount of the dominant juice in the recipe to account for the absence of syrup, or the drink will look a little short on the fill.

sugar cane, coarse brown sugar

flavoured sugar

It's funny how taste can evoke such potent memories. While recently tasting something, in spite of all the nostalgia it inspired, I drew a blank as to what it reminded me of... it was on the tip of my tongue! And then, all of a sudden, I was a kid again dipping lollypops into bags of orange-flavoured sugar.

That zing that keeps you coming back for more is a zesty combination of jelly sugar citric acid and baking soda.

flavoured sugar - recipe

Makes 100g / 3½oz or approximately 15 rimmed glasses
1 packet or 90g / 3oz flavoured jelly crystals
1 teaspoon citric acid
1 teaspoon baking soda

flavoured sugar - method

Grind all ingredients in a mortar and pestle until they become a powder. Alternatively, add ingredients to a dry blender or food processor and blend for 10 seconds.

Place flavoured sugar in a paper bag. Flavoured sugar keeps for up to three weeks, in a cool, dry cupboard away from sunlight, sealed in a paper- or resealable, snap-lock bag.

Here are a few of my favourite sugar flavourings:
lemon and/or lime
mango and passionfruit
pineapple
raspberry
reconstituted apple tea granuals - these can be found in specialty tea shops. They're basically apple, water and sugar boiled until they turn into apple-flavoured sugar crystals.

rimming glasses - why do it?

Rimming glasses on one hand can make a drink look appealing and make you as the creator, feel like you have mixed up a masterpiece. But the main reason why drinks have anything on the rim is to alter the flavour slightly, add texture to the drinking experience and also provide an option for the drinker to take as little or more of the desired rimming ingredient that they like. For example, you could half rim a margarita glass with salt if your guest only wanted a little salt. In the case of a sour drink where sugar can be an optional rimming ingredient, should the drinker like it sweet, they can take large gulps with large mouthfuls of sugar. And for those who like it sour, less or no sugar can be taken with the slurp of the cocktail.

rimming glasses - method

Decide on the adhesive ingredient to go with the rimming ingredient. In the case of ingredients like salt, finely crushed nuts or sugar plus more lightly textured ingredients use lime wheels at the base. If you choose to use more heavily textured ingredients such as chopped nuts or desiccated coconut, spread honey around in a saucer so the glass rim can be easily dipped in. Although honey is sweet in flavour, more textured ingredients will stick and not fall off and make a mess of a drink.

Carefully coat the rim of glass in the adhesive ingredient. Where lime is called for, cut three lime wheels and press the rim of glass in and turn to evenly coat.

Gently press the coated rim of glass into a saucer filled with rimming ingredient. Move the glass in circular movement to evenly coat the rim.

Note: Using a chilled glass before rimming and then being quick with the rimming method will yield a good clean result. Rimming the glass and then chilling the glass will often break up the rimmed ingredient and make the effect look messy.

citrus rind

Citrus rind is a good-looking garnish that is easy to prepare. You may also like to try sugar coated rind.

sugar coated citrus rind - method

Citrus rind can be cut by using a knife as opposed to the rind cutter as shown. Long rinds can be curled by wrapping them on the handle of a spoon and storing on ice for two minutes – this gives a very groovy spiral effect. One lemon yields 5 rind garnishes.

Place honey and sugar in two plates side by side, roll strips of citrus peel or rind in honey and then sugar. Put finished peels on baking paper before placing in a re-sealable container and storing in fridge.

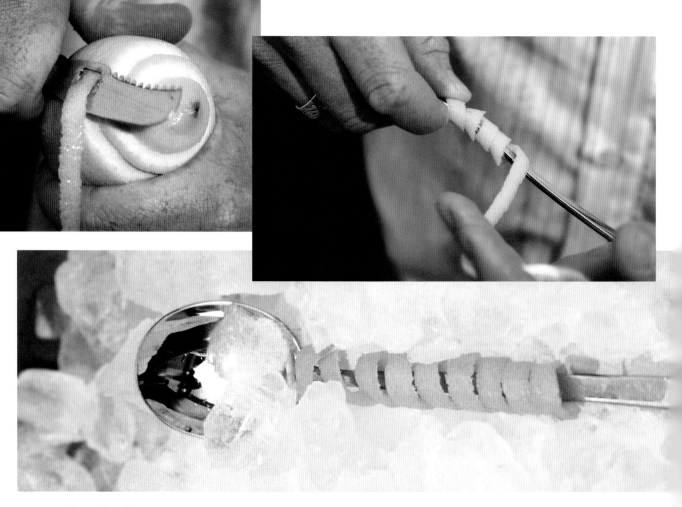

cocktail can seal - method

Once all ingredients have been added to your stainless steel cocktail shaker, make a boston cocktail shaker by fitting a mixing glass over the top of the cocktail shaker to form a tight seal. Make a true seal, ensuring a seam is formed with a flush connection on one side of the join.

The best way to ensure a true seal is to rub your hand up the side of the two units when joined to ensure there isn't a gap.

A false seal of a boston cocktail shaker is when there is a gap between the mixing glass and shaker all the way around the two units as they join. A false seal is much harder to separate and is a common cause of the mixing glass breaking.

To seperate the boston, hold either end and gently tap boston on the edge of your kitchen bench below glass seal.

muddle, shake and strain

Muddling is a popular method of drink mixing because the resulting flavour is exceptional. Muddling refers to extracting ingredients' raw flavours by crushing them with a big rolling pin or muddling stick. These flavours are then exaggerated with sugar and mixed with alcohol to make a vibrant drink which just bursts with flavour. The most famous example is of course the Mojito (see page 343) but you can make other great drinks using this method, such as Watermelon Shiver on page 72.

Be careful to note the instructions in recipes. After being shaken with ice, some drinks call for muddled ingredients to be poured straight back into the glass unstrained; others require straining using a hawthorne strainer; and others require double-straining with a hawthorne strainer and a small, fine sieve.

The results vary according to texture and method, and each suits a particular glass. For example, an unstrained muddled drink suits an old-fashioned glass or highball, whereas a strained muddled drink could also be served in a cocktail glass. Double-straining is most commonly used in drinks served without ice and in cocktail or martini glasses. The absence of textured fruit pulp in such drinks allows a more pure taste sensation when drinking and thus works much better in a more delicate glass.

muddle - method

Using a large rolling pin or muddling stick, firmly crush ingredients in base of mixing glass to extract ingredients' essential flavours and oils. Make a juicy mash, then add ice and alcohol.

shake and strain - method

Holding the boston cocktail shaker high, and ensuring you have a firm grip on either end, shake vigorously until you are satisfied everything is mixed well, usually around 5 seconds of shaking. Pour cocktail into glass by straining with a hawthorne strainer.

stir and strain - method

Fill mixing glass with ice and add listed ingredients. With a long spoon, knife or stirrer vigorously stir ingredients while holding a hand over the rim of the glass to prevent spillage. To complete cocktail mixing, fix a hawthorne strainer to rim of glass and strain off ice, and in some cases solids like fruit pulp, revealing an ultra-cold, well-mixed beverage.

double strain - method

Use a small, fine sieve in addition to the cocktail shaker's hawthorne strainer to strain ingredients into a glass. Resting sieve on rim of glass, pour drink through hawthorne strainer into the sieve. Stir pulp in sieve with a teaspoon to enable all liquid to pass through. A tea strainer can work as a replacement for a small sieve. Often tea strainers have super fine mesh that will give a very good strain, but being super fine they will also prolong this stage of the method as the liquid will strain slower.

blend

Blending is one of the most basic and important methods for anyone who wants to mix a few drinks. The trick to consistently good frozen blended drinks is to fill a glass with ice, and add this to the blender along with the other listed ingredients (leaving the glass out, of course!).

blend - method

Where fruit is listed, add this first to the blender cup as it will ease the blades into the ice. Add other listed ingredients, and finish with a glassful of ice from the glass that the drink will be served in. This not only chills the glass before blending, but ensures you have the right amount of ice.

Never use the glass to scoop the ice - if any glass ends up in the ice, you'll have to throw the lot away. And if any ends up in a guest's throat…

Rather than a whirlpool, look for a folding motion of the ingredients in the blender. To gain the required consistency add a few ice cubes at a time if needed and keep blending.

When pouring up more than one drink from a blender, always pour the first half way and then the others the same. Then evenly distribute the remaining blended drink to fill half filled glasses. This means everyone will get the same amount in the glass - short pours are often a result of the first drink being filled to the rim of the glass.

dusting - method

To create a patterned cocoa effect on top of drink balance straws on the rim of glass in desired pattern. Using either a cocoa shaker or a quarter teaspoon of cocoa dropped into a sieve, evenly cover the drink and straws with a dusting of cocoa.

Remove straws carefully to reveal the desired patter. If you like you can cut out shapes from card board to create unique designs to suit your party.

This garnish makes any creamy drink look impressive, but be sure to use it on drinks that are quite flat and not with a lot of texture.

skewered fruit fan

On my travels, I've found it the custom in many European nightclubs and bars to provide bowls of fruit with drinks. It's inspired me to use skewered fruit as a garnish in many of my own drinks recipes. It doesn't just look brilliant; it's also a tasty and healthy little morsel on the side.

skewered fruit fan - method

It's best to use crisp fruit like apples or crunchy pears when preparing these garnishes as they hold their fan shape better. Softer fruits like ripe mango loosen up and can droop.

Slice fruit lengthways in half from top to bottom. Then slice thinly from edge near skin to centre near core, keeping slices together. Stack 3-4 slices of fruit on top of each other then skewer pieces with wooden skewer. Fan slices out evenly over rim of glass and then place on top or in drink. For example see Fujini on pages 56 and 58.

For larger fruits like watermelon, cut fruit into thicker pieces and use less slices. The idea is to offer a complementary morsel that goes with the drink.

mixers

Mixers are an essential part of keeping drinks consistent. As with the other ideas and methods mentioned throughout the rest of the book, it's an excellent idea to prepare your mixers ahead of time. You don't want to have to mix your mixers as you mix your guests their drinks! Preparing your mixers in advance will take a lot of the complication out of the mixing, free up more space on the mixing station, and let you get on with getting everyone a drink!

sweet 'n' sour mix

This is a critical ingredient in most cocktail bars. As its name suggests, it adds a consistently sweet and sour flavour to drinks. It saves time when mixing drinks like Daiquiris, Margaritas or Sours (see page 331) in the Twenty-Five Classic Cocktails chapter. Preparing in advance a mixer like sweet 'n' sour mix, frees up time and space at a party for more important things like drinking the drinks you're mixing.

Makes 1Lt / 33½oz, (1 bottle) or approximately 16 drinks
250ml / 8½oz fresh lemon or lime juice
750ml / 25oz sugar syrup (see p 21)

Stir all ingredients in a jug or container. Keep sealed in fridge for up to two weeks.

Variations of sweet 'n' sour mix can include replacing lemon or lime juice with grapefruit or unsweetened freshly juiced orange juice. The sugar in the sugar syrup can also be replaced with any of the different sugars outlined in Sugar Daddy (see page 18). Sweet 'n' sour mix can be used as a substitute where fresh lemon or lime juice is followed immediately by sugar. Use it in drinks like Cezanne on page 71.

half 'n' half

Used as a replacement to pure cream, you'll find half 'n' half being used in many of the dessert drinks in Entrée and Dessert Cocktails on page 205 and the milkshakes in Coffees and Milkshakes on page 245. Using half measures of milk and cream to mix together is more versatile and much easier to drink - as well as on the waistline!

Makes 1Lt / 33½oz or approximately 16 drinks
500ml / 16½oz fresh milk
500ml / 16½oz fresh cream

Stir all ingredients in a jug or container. Store sealed in fridge for up to one week.

glazes

This combination of sugar, fruit-infused water or juice and a little alcohol makes a decadent glaze (stronger and thicker in consistency than a syrup). It's an excellent addition to any cocktail. Glazes' concentrated flavours enhance any mixed drink's flavour and appeal. If you've made a glaze from the recipes that follow, try using it in place of sugar syrup in drinks like Watermelon Shiver on page 72.

Glazes keep best out of the fridge. Keep them away from sunlight and preferably in a dark place like the pantry or kitchen cupboard.

Crystallised sugar may form on the inside of the bottle after a few days. This will probably be due to the size of the pot that stage one was boiled in. The larger the pot the more surface area the water has to boil. This results in more water evaporating during the hot infusion of the ingredients and thus, an over concentration of sugar in the recipe will give this crystallisation.

My old mate Pierre showed me this recipe and I owe him a big 'merci' for his great help in the kitchen and for bringing my ideas out of my brain and onto the page.

bottle sterilization - method

To sterilize a bottle, first clean and flush bottle with hot water to remove any sediment, stains or residue from the previous contents. Then carefully pour in heavily salted, diluted boiling water (2 tablespoons to 2L / 4 pts) to overfill the level of the bottle. This is best done in the sink to stop spills and burns. Leave salted water in bottle for 2 -3 minutes before emptying and flushing with hot water to remove excess salt.

Hot water on cold bottles can sometimes crack the bottle, so it's better to heat the bottle in hot water in the sink before pouring in boiling salted water.

glaze

glaze - recipe

Makes 600ml / 20oz or approximately 40 drinks

1kg / 2¼lb caster sugar

400ml / 14oz juice or fruit- infused water

60ml / 2oz alcohol

glaze - method

Making glazes with fruit-infused water is easy. To make fruit-infused water, just boil 500ml / 17½oz water with listed fruit or ingredients in a small pot for 30 minutes. Strain off solid ingredients.

Add sugar to fruit-infused water in pot and cook for a further 5 minutes over medium heat. Stir sugar into liquid and bring to the boil, then remove from heat.

Add alcohol and stir thoroughly through hot glaze. Allow to cool before bottling in a sterilized bottle.

Glazes keep best out of the fridge. Keep them away from sunlight and preferably in a dark place like the pantry or kitchen cupboard.

rum raisin glaze

Makes 600ml / 20oz or approximately 20 drinks

400ml / 14oz Ocean Spray Cranberry Classic juice

60ml / 2oz Havana Club Añejo Blanco rum

100ml / 3½oz red wine

1 cup raisins

2 cinnamon quills

10 cloves, whole

1kg / 2¼lb sugar

Boil cranberry juice and red wine in pot with raisins, cinnamon and cloves for 30 minutes. Strain off solid ingredients. Add sugar as outlined in basic method (see page 44). Add rum then cool for 30 minutes before bottling and sealing. Glaze will keep in a sterilized bottle in cupboard for 3-4 weeks.

pink pineapple glaze

Makes 600ml / 20oz or approximately 20 drinks

500ml / 17½oz water

2 thick slices pineapple, chopped

15ml / ½oz Angostura bitters

1kg - 2¼lb sugar

Boil water in pot with pineapple for 30 minutes. Strain off solid ingredients. Add sugar as outlined in basic method (see page 44). Add Angostura bitters then cool for 30 minutes before bottling and sealing. Glaze will keep in a sterilized bottle in cupboard for 3-4 weeks.

banana coconut glaze

Makes 600ml / 20oz or approximately 20 drinks

60ml / 2oz Havana Club Añejo Blanco rum

500ml / 17½oz water

2 bananas, peeled and chopped

1 cup desiccated coconut

1kg / 2¼lb sugar

Dry-roast coconut, in a small pot, for 5 minutes or until golden brown. Add banana and water then boil for 30 minutes. Strain off solid ingredients. Add sugar as outlined in basic method (see page 44). Add rum then cool for 30 minutes before bottling and sealing. Glaze will keep in a sterilized bottle in cupboard for 3-4 weeks.

orange ginger glaze

Makes 600ml / 20oz or approximately 20 drinks

60ml / 2oz 42 Below vodka

500ml / 17½oz water

2 oranges, zested

3 cm ginger root, diced

1kg / 2¼lb sugar

Boil water with orange zest and ginger for 30 minutes. Strain off solid ingredients. Add sugar as outlined in basic method (see page 44). Add vodka then cool for 30 minutes before bottling and sealing. Glaze will keep in a sterilized bottle in cupboard for 3-4 weeks.

apple, raspberry and vanilla glaze

Makes 600ml / 20oz or approximately 20 drinks

60ml / 2oz 42 Below vodka

500ml / 17½oz water

2 apples, cored and chopped

½ cup raspberries

1 vanilla bean, whole

1kg / 2¼lb sugar

Boil water in pot with apple, raspberries and vanilla for 30 minutes. Strain off solid ingredients. Add sugar as outlined in basic method (see page 44). Add vodka then cool for 30 minutes before bottling and sealing. Glaze will keep in a sterilized bottle in cupboard for 3-4 weeks.

grandberry glaze

Makes 600ml / 20oz or approximately 20 drinks

60ml / 2oz Grand Marnier

400ml / 13½oz Ocean Spray Cranberry Classic juice

100ml / 3½oz water

1kg / 2¼lb sugar

Boil cranberry juice and water for 15 minutes. Add sugar as outlined in basic method (see page 44). Add Grand Marnier then cool for 30 minutes before bottling and sealing. Glaze will keep in a sterilized bottle in cupboard for 3-4 weeks.

hipalicious

The venue was the Cave in the heart of Rome's nightlife district. I was on tour, guest-bartending at venues around the world. Rome was ablaze with talk of how, earlier that day, when he'd been discussing African debt with Bono of U2, the then Pope John Paul II had taken Bono's ubiquitous fly sunglasses and put them on himself. It must have been quite a sight.

The club was packed by 10.30pm and we were shaking. When I say shaking, I mean bottles flying, liquor pouring and music pumping. By midnight, the crowd was pumped and cheering for more. To really impress them, I set fire to the bar top and began a cocktail flair show to rival the Sistine Chapel: stacking the drinks higher and higher until I had ten piled up on top of each other on the bar. My then employers had flown in from Atlanta to see me at work, and I was giving them - and everyone else - the spectacle of their lives!

It was one of those moments, when the crowd's jumping, the music's going off, you're standing on a fiery bar top making a humungous cocktail sculpture, and everyone's calling your name, that you feel like a rock star.

And then Bono walked in.

They say really famous people radiate an energy that resonates out into the corner of every room. It's a vibe, something you can't quite explain - even though it's plain to see.

Everyone, including me, turned to look - and that was enough for my cocktail masterpiece to start swaying dangerously. It might have been Bono's vibe, a moment of distraction, or just a stray draft, but this wasn't supposed to be happening! What was supposed to be happening was that, Bono or not, I would put the finishing touches to the whole shebang with a flamboyant flourish, the crowd would cheer wildly and praise me for my impeccable skills in flair bartending, and my employers would be so impressed that they'd give me a raise on the spot.

But the fall of the Leaning Tower of Woody - ten full drinks hitting a concrete floor with an almighty crash - silenced them - and me. It's funny how loud silence can be in a packed nightclub. Suddenly, I felt very silly, standing on a now smouldering bar top, gazing on the ruins of my folly and my career - I was sure my boss would sack me for the wastage alone, let alone the embarrassment.

Suddenly a very loud and enthusiastic Yeeeeeaaaaahhhh! burst out of the VIP corner, followed by hearty Irish laughter. The whole crowd turned in surprise, and moments later, joined in, whooping and applauding. A DJ might not have saved my life that night, but a rock star with a sense of humour did! And the party suddenly went up a notch: it seemed to go on forever…

Many of the drinks in this chapter use three basic but important bartender tricks: muddling, shaking and building. Making a fool of yourself in front of rock royalty? That'll have to wait for another time…

leopold

If you're looking for a very cool drink to make and you don't have a great deal of time to make it then this is for you: a simple muddled cocktail with no glazes or syrups to prepare. This cocktail is sweet with a strong mango flavour base. The hint of spice from the cardamom mixed with the fresh kaffir gives the drink a zippy citrus-perfumed lift.

Makes 1 drink
60ml / 2oz Havana Club Añejo Blanco Rum
30ml / 1oz Ocean Spray White Cranberry juice
60ml / 2oz mango nectar
2 fresh kaffir lime leaves
2 cardamom pods
2 teaspoons caster sugar
skewered mango fan, to garnish (see p 39)
ice

Muddle fresh kaffir lime leaves and cardamom in base of mixing glass with sugar, then add remaining ingredients. Shake and double-strain into a chilled cocktail glass. Garnish with skewered mango fan. See pages 30 and 33 for more on muddling, shaking and double-straining.

muscato

This is a smooth and rich tasting cocktail - almost like a liquid Christmas mince pie. It draws on muscat grapes for its sophisticated flavour, although it can still be enjoyed with any variety of grape as an alternative.

Makes 1 drink

30ml / 1oz 42 Below vodka

30ml / 1oz South gin

60ml / 2oz Ocean Spray Cranberry Classic juice

30ml / 1oz rum raisin glaze (see p 46)

5 muscat grapes

¼ lime, chopped

lemon-flavoured sugar rim, to garnish (see p 22)

ice

Muddle muscat grapes, lime and glaze in base of mixing glass then add remaining ingredients. Shake and strain into a chilled martini glass. Garnish with lemon-flavoured sugar rim.

queen cameroon

I like using fresh kaffir lime leaves for a garnish. You can find them in any good supermarket or asian food market. If fresh kaffir lime leaves aren't available, an alternative is to use fresh citrus zest. Although not as delicate, the aroma and flavour is almost the same.

Makes 1 drink

45ml / 1¼oz Cuervo tequila

15ml / ½oz Midori

90ml / 3oz Ocean Spray White Cranberry juice

15ml / ½oz banana coconut glaze (see p 47)

1 lime wedge, squeezed

1 fresh kaffir lime leaf, to garnish

ice

Shake and double-strain ingredients into an ice-filled cocktail glass. Garnish with fresh kaffir lime leaf.

flying fox

Makes 1 drink

45ml / 1¼oz Havana Club Añejo Blanco rum

15ml / ½oz Campari

30ml / 1oz Lipton Lemon Herbal Infusion, steeped then chilled

60ml / 2oz sweet 'n' sour mix (see p 40)

raspberry-flavoured sugar rim, to garnish (see p 22, 25)

ice

Shake and strain ingredients into a chilled cocktail glass. Garnish with raspberry-flavoured sugar rim. See page 30 for more on shaking and straining.

fujini

I really like the Fujini's flavour balance. Crisp apple and a rich berry glaze, complemented by sparkling water.

Makes 1 drink

20ml / ¾oz South gin

20ml / ¾oz Grand Marnier

30ml / 1oz grandberry glaze (see p 48)

½ fuji apple, cored and chopped

sparkling water, to top

flavoured sugar rim, to garnish (see p 22)

skewered fuji apple fan, to garnish (see p 39)

ice

Muddle apple with glaze in base of mixing glass, then add remaining ingredients except sparkling water. Shake and double-strain into martini glass then top with sparkling water. Garnish with flavoured sugar rim and skewered apple fan. See pages 30 and 33 for more on muddling, shaking and double-straining.

lupino

The feijoa (FAY-hoe-ah) is an exotic South American relative of the guava. It tastes like a cross between a ripe pear and banana, with a citrus/lime finish. 42 Below Feijoa vodka continues 42 Below's continued innovation with flavoured vodkas. You can find them in any good liquor outlet - but if you can't, just use your own favourite flavoured or infused vodkas or add fresh feijoas. For more on infusing vodka, see page 164.

Makes 1 drink

30ml / 1oz Cuervo tequila

30ml / 1oz 42 Below Feijoa vodka

60ml / 2oz Lipton Flavoured Black Tea Honeycomb, steeped then chilled

30ml / 1oz grandberry glaze (see p 48)

4 raspberries

1 raspberry, speared, to garnish

ice

Shake and strain all ingredients into a cocktail glass. Garnish with speared raspberry.

honey rose ambrosia

This is a deluxe cocktail you could expect from a world class cocktail bar but can enjoy in the comfort of your own home. If you take the time to make the orange ginger glaze, you'll be stunned by the final result.

Makes 1 drink

30ml / 1oz 42 Below Feijoa vodka

30ml / 1oz Grand Marnier

15ml / ½oz orange ginger glaze (see p 47)

5ml / ¼oz rose water

30ml / 1oz Lipton Green Tea with Honey, steeped then chilled

rose petals, to garnish

ice

Shake and strain into an ice-filled highball glass. Garnish with rose petals.

flying fox, fujini, lupino, honey rose ambrosia

spindarella

This is a drink that's all about the pineapple. So tropical and smooth, it's sweet and perfect for relaxing by the pool. A breezy, summery, fun cocktail.

Makes 1 drink

45ml / 1½oz Cuervo tequila

15ml / ½oz Midori

60ml / 2oz pineapple juice

5 dashes Angostura bitters

15ml / ½oz pink pineapple glaze (see p 46)

Piper-Heidsieck champagne, to top

thin slice of pineapple and pineapple leaf, to garnish

ice

Shake and strain over ice in highball glass. Garnish with thin slice of pineapple and pineapple leaf.

ramos

It's important to muddle ingredients thoroughly, especially in this refreshing and aromatic cocktail. Extracting all the goodness from the mint and lime will ensure a standout result.

Makes 1 drink

60ml / 2oz 42 Below vodka

30ml / 1oz Ocean Spray White Cranberry juice

½ lime, chopped

10 mint leaves

1 teaspoon caster sugar

Piper-Heidsieck champagne, to top

ice

Muddle lime and mint in base of mixing glass with sugar, then add remaining ingredients. Shake and pour unstrained into an old-fashioned glass. Top with champagne.

esmeralda and woody tag-team delicious ramos cocktails

jive

Coriander and ginger add spicy characters to a drink. A great way to keep you and your taste buds jiving all night long.

Makes 1 drink

60ml / 2oz Havana Club Añejo Blanco rum

30ml / 1oz Lipton Lemon Herbal Infusion, steeped and chilled

½ lime, chopped

1 tablespoon coriander, chopped

1 teaspoon ginger, chopped

2 teaspoons caster sugar

slice ginger (3 cm), julienne, to garnish

1 fresh kaffir lime leaf, to garnish

crushed ice

Muddle lime, coriander and ginger in base of mixing glass with sugar, then add remaining ingredients. Shake and pour unstrained into an old-fashioned glass. Garnish with ginger chopped julienne and fresh kaffir lime leaf. See page 30 for more on muddling and shaking.

zoogogo

Makes 1 drink

30ml / 1oz Cuervo tequila

30ml / 1oz Midori

30ml / 1oz Ocean Spray White Cranberry Peach juice

30ml / 1oz mango nectar

30ml / 1oz grandberry glaze (see p 48)

lime wheels, to garnish

crushed ice

Add grandberry glaze to base of cocktail glass and fill with ice. Shake remaining ingredients, then strain into cocktail glass. Garnish with lime wheels. See page 30 for more on shaking and straining.

jazzball

Makes 1 drink

20ml / ¾oz Cuervo tequila

20ml / ¾oz Campari

20ml / ¾oz Grand Marnier

60ml / 2oz Ocean Spray White Cranberry Peach juice

sparkling water, to top

lemon zest, to garnish

crushed ice

Shake and strain into a chilled cocktail glass. Garnish with lemon zest. See page 33 for more on straining.

ra

Makes 1 drink

45ml / 1 ½oz Remy Martin Grand Cru cognac

15ml / ½oz Campari

30ml / 1oz passionfruit pulp

15ml / ½oz orange ginger glaze (see p 47)

sparkling water, to top

sugar coated orange rind, to garnish (see p 26)

ice

Build ingredients over crushed ice in highball glass. Garnish with sugar coated orange rind.

scuba spark

Makes 1 drink

45ml / 15oz 42 Below Passionfruit vodka

15ml / ½oz Midori

30ml / 1oz Ocean Spray Cranberry Black Currant juice

15ml / ½oz grandberry glaze (see p 48)

sparkling water, to top

speared blueberries, to garnish

ice

Starting with grandberry glaze, build ingredients over crushed ice in highball glass. Garnish with speared blueberries. If blueberries aren't available, substitute grapes.

picnic margarita

The convenience of using ready prepared sweeteners like golden syrup in a cocktail not only adds to the ease of preparation, using different varieties like maple, honey or golden syrup make for great alternative flavours.

Makes 1 drink

45ml / 1½oz Cuervo tequila

15ml / ½oz Midori

60ml / 2oz Ocean Spray Ruby Red Grapefruit juice

½ fresh lime, chopped

4 table grapes

1 teaspoon golden syrup

crushed salted pistachio nut rim, to garnish (see p 25)

crushed ice

Muddle lime and grapes in base of mixing glass with golden syrup. Add remaining ingredients then shake and pour unstrained into an old-fashioned glass. Garnish with crushed salted pistachio rim. See page 30 for more on muddling.

ra, scuba spark

kazooni

Makes 1 drink

30ml / 1oz Remy Martin Grand Cru cognac

30ml / 1oz Lipton Lemon Herbal Infusion, steeped then chilled

60ml / 2oz Piper-Heidsieck champagne

30ml / 1oz orange ginger glaze (see p 47)

orange rind, to garnish

mango-flavoured sugar rim, to garnish (see p 22)

crushed ice

Build ingredients over ice in cocktail glass and stir. Garnish with orange rind and mango-flavoured sugar rim. If you don't have mango jelly crystals, try any flavour you like.

To make citrus fruit rind is a simple but effective garnish. It is done by peeling skin from the fruit with a rinder or paring knife (a small sharp knife with a short blade) in a long strip between 1cm wide and 5-8cm long. Angle cut each end to make a clean finish and curl around a chopstick or spoon to create a twist. Placing the curled rind on ice will set the rind, prolonging the curled effect.

cezanne

Makes 1 drink

60ml / 2oz 42 Below vodka

60ml / 2oz Ocean Spray Cranberry Black Currant juice

5 dashes Angostura bitters

30ml / 1oz sweet 'n' sour mix (see p 40)

30ml / 1oz rum raisin glaze (see p 46)

sugar coated lemon zest, to garnish (see p 26)

ice

Shake all ingredients in an ice-filled cocktail shaker. Strain and pour into a chilled martini glass. Garnish with sugar coated lemon zest. See page 33 for more on straining.

watermelon shiver

Watermelon is without doubt one of the most refreshing fruits, especially so in summer when it's also at its sweetest. However, you can also use red table grapes and a dash of Ocean Spray Ruby Red Grapefruit juice if you want to try something different or can't use watermelon. Experiment with substitutions and play around with the ingredients for different variations and taste sensations.

Makes 1 drink
45ml / 1 ½oz South gin
15ml / ½oz Campari
30ml / 1oz rum raisin glaze (see p 46)
5 (2 cm) watermelon chunks
skewered watermelon slices, to garnish
crushed ice

Muddle watermelon and run 'n' raisin glaze in mixing glass then add remaining ingredients. Shake and double-strain (see page 33) over crushed ice in a cocktail glass. Garnish with two skewered watermelon slices. See page 30 for more on muddling.

rivendell

This drink is inspired by the Falling Water, the signature cocktail of the world famous Mattehorn bar in Wellington New Zealand. The Mattehorn was the preferred tavern for the hobbits, dwarfs, wizards and other assorted cast and crew who worked on the Lord of the Rings trilogy during filming. The Falling Water consists of 42 Below Feijoa vodka and a large slice of cucumber in highball glass, topped with Chi herbal sparkling water. I hope this fresh potion is a worthy tribute.

Makes 1 drink
30ml / 1oz Remy Martin Grand Cru cognac
30ml / 1oz 42 Below Feijoa vodka
120ml / 4oz clear lemonade
1 large cucumber slice, to garnish
crushed ice

Build over ice in highball glass. Garnish with cucumber slice.

crimson del monico

Makes 1 drink
45ml / 1½oz 42 Below vodka
15ml / ½oz Cuervo tequila
60ml / 2oz Ocean Spray Ruby Red Grapefruit juice
30ml / 1oz sweet 'n' sour mix (see p 40)
5 dashes Angostura bitters
½ teaspoon rose water
sugar coated citrus rind, to garnish (see p 26)
ice

Shake all ingredients and pour strained into a chilled cocktail glass. Garnish with sugar coated citrus rind. See page 33 for more on shaking and straining.

throwing punches

Having been invited to a few parties in my time, I've been to my fair share of crackers where everybody had a great time - and shockers where it felt as if we were all on our first blind date set up by our mothers. Parties where the host is stressed out make everyone else feel awkward or tense as well. Not very conducive to a party mood! The trick to throwing a successful party is to ensure everyone has a good time, and the best way to do that is to ensure that you've prepared in advance and taken a chill pill so that all your guests feel welcome and relaxed.

Having said that, even when the furniture's been moved out of the way, and the stereo's been beefed up with enough wattage to make the neighbours call the police before a tune's been played, and there's enough alcohol to turn a boatload of thirsty sailors teetotal… well, the worst part of any party - even worse than the next day - is the hour before: the gnashies. This is the terrible hour when you gnash your teeth, wondering if anyone will turn up. Did you send out enough invites? Did you remember to remind them? Maybe they'll forget? Maybe they don't really like you… you know the feeling. I hate the gnashies.

So, if you do happen to be amongst the first to arrive, apart from giving your poor gnashied-out host a cuddle, why not throw them a punch? Not one involving your fist, but a big bowl and lots of cups.
It's said that the word punch comes from the Hindustani word 'panch', meaning 'five'. Not five fingers, just lots of goodies that pack a punch!

This is why I like to turn up first to parties, none of this fashionably late stuff. I'll raid the liquor cabinet and bash out a punch that everyone can have a slug of when they walk in the door. This is a sure way of keeping the party going and keeping everyone friends all night.

In this chapter I have explored some very old-styled drinks, some that go back thousands of years.

nut milk

The two punches that follow are very old traditional punches that use nut milk. Nut milk is made by softening unsalted nuts like cashews or almonds in boiling water. Then blending the water and nuts to impart with flavour and colour.

nut milk - method

Once ingredients have been cooked and cooled then blended, line the inside of a bowl with a clean tea-towel. Pour the ingredients into the tea towel then wrap up the contents. Twist the ends of the towel to tighten the nut milk mixture. Keep twisting the towel to squeeze the nut milk into the bowl until the contents are dry.

Discard the nutmeal or, if you don't like waste, find a recipe in your favourite baking cookbook and bake biscuits or muffins with it.

orange and almond nectar

This is a traditional Jewish recipe given to me by the Mender family in Israel many years ago. I used to work on their farm and every Friday they generously invited me to Shabbat dinner (a traditional family meal held on the eve of the Sabbath). It's simple and yet refreshingly moreish.

Makes 2L / 4 pints, or approximately 13 drinks
370ml / 12oz freshly juiced orange juice
1.5L / 3 pints water
1 cup raw unsalted almonds
¾ cup caster sugar
ice (optional)

In a saucepan, simmer almonds with 1L water for ½ hour. Allow to cool before blending for 2 minutes until mixture has become creamy. Add remaining 500ml water and blend for 1 minute. Strain using basic nut milk straining method. Adding freshly juiced orange juice and caster sugar, stir well in a bowl or jug. Serve cold with or without ice in highball glasses.

anise, fruit and nut brunch punch

This is a very popular morning drink in India called Thandhai. It is said to soothe and cool the body and soul before the day begins.

Makes 2L / 4 pints, or approximately 13 drinks

500ml / 1 pints fresh milk

1.5L / 3 pints cold water

15ml / ½oz rose water

1 cup caster sugar

½ cup sultanas

½ cup raw unsalted cashews

5 whole green cardamom pods

10 whole black peppercorns (optional)

2 tablespoons anise seeds (you may substitute star anise or fennel seeds)

In a saucepan, simmer 1 Litre / 2 pints water with cashew nuts, sultanas, cardamom, pepper and anise seeds for ½ hour. Allow to cool before blending for 2 minutes until mixture has become creamy. Add remaining 500ml / 1 pint water and blend for 1 minute. Strain using basic nut milk straining method (see p 78). Once strained, add sugar, rosewater and milk before chilling. Serve without ice in highball glasses.

jerusalem lemonade

Lemonade is always refreshing. My dad has his recipe, and so does pretty much every other dad I know. Here's one I remember being poured as if the recipe hadn't changed for a thousand years in and amongst the hustle and bustle of old Jerusalem.

I was taught this recipe by a guy who ran a falafel stand just inside the Muslim Quarter of old Jerusalem. His fantastic lemonade was always served very cold and quenched the thirst of another hot Middle Eastern summer. It was also the perfect chaser to wonderful falafels in fresh pitta bread, served with tomato and cucumber yoghurt.

Makes 1.5L / 3 pints, or approximately 10 drinks
90ml / 3oz fresh lemon juice
15ml / ½oz orange blossom water
½ cup caster sugar
10 mint leaves, finely chopped
1 small mint sprig per glass, to garnish
1.25L / 2½ pints sparkling water
ice

Blend all ingredients, except sparkling water, until sugar has dissolved. Add sparkling water and stir in a large jug, then chill. Serve over ice in old-fashioned glasses. Garnish with mint. For another lemonade recipe try Cambodian Lemonade in the Waters chapter, see page 328.

Orange blossom water can usually be found next to rose water in the baking ingredients aisle of any good supermarket; but if it's unavailable, try orange essence instead.

salsita punch

This is a great aperitif-style punch, best enjoyed before dinner. It's a good idea to strain the watermelon juice well as the bubbles in the champagne will separate the pulp from the juice, creating sediment that some may not find appealing. But it still tastes fantastic! See page 103 in the Juicing and Blending chapter for more on juicing pulp.

Makes 1L / 2 pints, or approximately 6 drinks
750ml / 23½oz Piper-Heidsieck Champagne
370ml / 12oz watermelon juice (see pages 35 and 134 for more on blending)
1 cup caster sugar
10 dashes Angostura bitters
1 chunky watermelon slice per glass, to garnish
ice

Stir watermelon, sugar and Angostura bitters in jug until sugar dissolves. Chill. When ready, pour chilled champagne into jug. Serve over ice in old-fashioned glasses. Garnish with chunky watermelon slices.

cranberry and strawberry spider

Makes 3L / 6 pints, or approximately 18 drinks
1L / 2 pints Ocean Spray White Cranberry Strawberry juice
1 punnet strawberries, pruned and blended
½ cup caster sugar
500ml / 1 pint lemonade
1 scoop vanilla ice cream per glass
½ cup chocolate chips, to garnish
1 punnet strawberries, chopped, to garnish

Stir all ingredients except ice cream in large bowl until sugar is dissolved. Scoop ice cream into highball glasses then pour over punch mix. Garnish with chocolate chips and chopped strawberries.

custo punch

Makes 2L / 4 pints, or approximately 13 drinks

100ml / 1 ½oz Midori

100ml / 1 ½oz Grand Marnier

185ml / 6oz Ocean Spray White Cranberry juice

185ml / 6oz mango nectar

1 cup caster sugar

2 x 750ml / 25oz bottles Piper-Heidsieck champagne

1 green mango, julienned, to garnish

Stir juice, sugar and liqueurs in jug until sugar dissolves. Chill with champagne flutes. When ready, pour chilled champagne into jug and serve in chilled champagne flutes. Garnish with julienne green mango.

honey punch

Makes 2L / 4 pints, or approximately 13 drinks

100ml / 1 ½oz 42 Below Manuka Honey vodka

100ml / 1 ½oz Grand Marnier

185ml / 6oz Ocean Spray Cranberry Classic juice

185ml / 6oz apricot nectar

1 cup caster sugar

2 x 750ml / 25oz bottles Piper-Heidsieck champagne

2 limes, sliced, to garnish

Stir juice, sugar, vodka and liqueur in jug until sugar dissolves. Chill with champagne flutes. When ready, pour chilled champagne into jug and serve in chilled champagne flutes. Garnish with lime slices.

woody gets into making custo punch

sparkling white sangria

No matter how hard people try to tell you they make the best, sangrìa is by its very nature - along with almost every other punch recipe - a combination of ingredients that will be hard if not impossible to replicate in flavour each and every time. That's what I like about it!

Sangrìa is a red wine-based punch and its variations throughout Spain suggest that it would be unrealistic to pronounce a standard recipe. Sangria is a derivative of the word sangre which means blood. Not that the Spanish drink blood, but good sangrìa is the colour of blood (which means that the base ingredient, red wine, is good quality).

Although the name, white sangrìa is contradictory, any wine-based punch can be called sangrìa. This sparkling white sangrìa uses some of the base flavours commonly found in Spanish sangrìa like cinnamon and cloves. It's quite a tasty difference.

Makes 2L / 4 pints, or approximately 13 drinks
185ml / 6oz Havana Club Añejo Blanco rum
90ml / 3oz Grand Marnier
1L / 2 pints Ocean Spray White Cranberry juice
750ml / 25oz Piper-Heidsieck champagne
90ml / 3oz sugar syrup (see p 21)
4 cinnamon quills
2 teaspoons cloves
12 orange slices, to garnish

Stir juice, sugar syrup, spices and liqueur in a large jug until sugar dissolves. Chill with champagne glasses. When ready, pour chilled champagne into jug and serve over ice in small wine glasses.

picnic margarita punch

Instead of salt on the rim of a glass to complement the tang of a Margarita, try crushed salted pistachio nuts. Not only does it add a tasty crunch, it'll be the talking point at your picnic. Shell 50g of salted pistachios then crush them in a mortar and pestle. Alternatively, you may grind them in a coffee grinder or food processor - or even place them in a tea towel and give them a good bash!

Makes 2L / 4 pints, or approximately 13 drinks
180ml / 6oz Cuervo tequila
90ml / 3oz Midori
1L / 2 pints Ocean Spray Ruby Red Grapefruit juice
500ml / 1 pint grape juice (still or sparkling)
185ml / 9oz sugar syrup (see p 21)
90ml / 3oz lime juice
2 limes cut into wheels, to garnish
ground pistachio rim, to garnish
ice

Stir all ingredients in large bowl then chill. Serve over ice in old-fashioned glasses. Garnish with lime wheels and ground pistachio rim.

To rim a glass adds a great look to a drink, which is sure to impress. For sugar or salt, rub the rim of the glass with a slice of lemon or lime and dip in the ingredient for rimming. For more textured ingredients like coconut or ground nuts you might like to use honey for a stickier rim. For more on Margaritas, see the Margarita recipe on page 341 of the Twenty-Five Classic Cocktails chapter.

punch up

white peach and mandarin rum punch

Makes 3L / 6 pints, or approximately 18 drinks

300ml / 10oz Havana Club Añejo Blanco rum

1L / 2 pints Ocean Spray White Cranberry Peach juice

8 mandarins juiced

¾ cup caster sugar

1.25L / 2½ pints sparkling water

2 mandarins cut into wheels, to garnish

ice

Stir all ingredients in large bowl then chill. Serve over ice in highball glasses. Garnish with mandarin wheels.

hot egg nog

Hot egg nog is one of those drinks that's made for a cold day. Find someone you'd like to snuggle up with. Put on a pot of egg nog and hold out until the storm blows over. It warms the hands and the soul. It tastes like slightly spiced vanilla custard and therefore, the whole experience works well with a small bowl of ice cream on the side. Egg nog and ice cream is a hot and cold taste sensation. It's also a hot conversation lubricant. Who can't help feeling cosy?

peace out

hot egg nog - method

Makes 2L / 4 pints, or approximately 13 drinks

300ml / 10oz Remy Martin Grand Cru cognac

1.5L / 3 pints milk

4 eggs

2 tablespoons vanilla extract

½ cup caster sugar

2 teaspoons nutmeg

nutmeg dusting, to garnish

Whisk eggs in large pot until peaked and fluffy. Whisk all ingredients together until sugar is dissolved. Heat over low heat for 5-10 minutes and stir continuously. Garnish with nutmeg dusting.

napkin wrap - method

This is a good way to ensure people don't burn their fingers on a hot glass.

Unfold a paper napkin on a flat surface so it's completely open and flat. Fold into 2-3 cm folds to make a single long strip. Taking a glass turned upside down, fit napkin around base, joining ends with your fingers, folding one end over and under the other end, turning it back on itself like a knot. Repeat for other end. Press the join flush against glass and slide wrap towards rim.

foxy blossom punch, marmalade margarita punch, all spice apple, orange punch

foxy blossom punch

Makes 3L / 6 pints, or approximately 18 drinks

500ml / 1 pint 42 Below vodka

2L / 4 pints Ocean Spray Cranberry Classic juice

185ml / 6oz fresh lemon juice

1 cup caster sugar

15ml / ½oz orange blossom water

20 fresh mint leaves, finely chopped, to garnish

2 oranges cut into wheels, to garnish

ice

Stir all ingredients in large bowl then chill. Serve over ice in old-fashioned glasses. Garnish with mint and orange wheels.

marmalade margarita punch

Makes 2L / 4 pints, or approximately 13 drinks

300ml / 10oz Cuervo tequila

200ml / 6½oz Midori

1L / 2 pints mango nectar

200g / 6½oz marmalade

90ml / 3oz maple syrup

200ml / 6½oz fresh lime juice or 4 limes juiced

2 limes cut into wheels, to garnish

Blend marmalade, maple and lime juice until marmalade has dissolved. Stir together with other ingredients in a large jug then chill. Serve over ice in old-fashioned glasses. Garnish with lime wedges.

allspice, apple, orange punch

Makes 3L / 6 pints, or approximately 18 drinks

12 apples juiced or 1L / 2 pints cloudy apple juice

12 oranges, juiced or 1.5L / 3 pints freshly juiced orange juice

½ cup caster sugar

2 teaspoons allspice, ground

20 mint leaves, finely chopped

2 apples, sliced, to garnish

orange rind, to garnish (see p 26)

ice

Stir all ingredients in large bowl until sugar is dissolved. Chill. Serve over ice in highball glasses. Garnish with apple slices and orange rind.

golden gimlet punch

A gimlet is a sweet, gin-based drink, traditionally made with the addition of lime cordial and a slice of fresh lime.

Makes 2L / 4 pints, or approximately 13 drinks

300ml / 10oz South gin

200ml / 6½oz Midori

1.5L / 3 pints Ocean Spray White Cranberry Peach juice

90ml / 3oz golden syrup

2 peaches, sliced into wheels, to garnish

1 cup cherries

ice

Stir all ingredients in large bowl until syrup is dissolved. Chill. Serve over ice in old-fashioned glasses. Garnish with a peach slice and cherry.

spiced gypsy punch

The spiced gypsy punch uses white wine and mango along with spice and rum to change the mood at you next tapas festival.

Makes 3L / 6 pints, or approximately 18 drinks
180ml / 6oz Havana Club Añejo Blanco rum
1.5 / 3 pints Ocean Spray White Cranberry juice
1L / 2 pints white wine
500ml / 1 pint mango nectar
1 cup caster sugar
3 cinnamon quills
1 mango, sliced with skin left on, to garnish
ice

Stir all ingredients in large bowl then chill. Serve over ice in old-fashioned glasses. Garnish with mango slices.

seville sangrìa

Makes 2L / 4 pints, or approximately 13 drinks
300ml / 10oz Havana Club Añejo Blanco rum
90ml / 3oz Grand Marnier
700ml / 23 ½oz dry red wine
500ml / 1 pint apple juice
300ml / 10oz sugar syrup (see p 21)
2 cinnamon quills
1 blood orange chopped julienne, to garnish
ice

Stir all ingredients in a large jug. Serve over ice in any kind of glass.

pineapple and coconut punch

This is a light twist on the Piña Colada without the heaviness of coconut and full cream. Condensed milk is a lovely way to 'cream up a drink' and sweeten it without relying on too much of the heavy stuff. A great pool party punch.

Makes 3L / 6 pints, or approximately 18 drinks

500ml / 1 pint Havana Club Añejo Blanco rum

2 pineapples juiced or 2L / 4 pints pineapple juice

90ml / 3oz sweetened condensed milk

15ml / ½oz coconut essence

¼ cup caster sugar

500ml / 1 pint sparkling water

3 mint sprigs, to garnish

Blend all ingredients except mint, sparkling water and ice. Chill in the fridge until cold. Once chilled add sparkling water and stir. Serve in old-fashioned glasses. Garnish with fresh mint.

mango and coconut punch

Makes 3L / 6 pints, or approximately 18 drinks

500ml / 1 pint Cuervo tequila

2L / 4 pints mango nectar

90ml / 3oz sweetened condensed milk

15ml / ½oz coconut essence

¼ cup caster sugar

500ml / 1 pint lemonade

orange rind, to garnish

Stir all ingredients in large bowl until condensed milk is dissolved. Chill in the fridge until cold. Serve in ice-filled old-fashioned glasses. Garnish with orange rind.

juicing and
blending

It's always important to understand what effect the things you put into your body will have on you. Yes, I'm a bartender, and yes, you may have noticed I like to enjoy a cocktail now and then - but as well as my unhealthy obsession with my cocktail shaker and muddling stick, I also have a very healthy obsession with my juicer and blender.

Everyone these days seems to be flocking to health spas, alternative therapists, nutritionists, organic markets and health food stores - let alone juice bars, which seem to be everywhere! But even if you don't have a juicer, you might like to use these recipes and adapt them with the muddling method (see page 30). The result will of course be different but it's my stand on things like this, that recipes are simply a guide to inspiration; you must add or subtract, change or alter recipes to suit yourself and what ingredients (or in this case equipment) you have available.

the juicer

As you've probably noticed, throughout this book, the basic building block for many recipes is lemon or lime and freshly juiced orange juice - in sweet 'n' sour mix (see page 40) and in many of the drinks that follow in this chapter. Its lively tartness invigorates almost any drink but as anyone who's had to squeeze citrus juice manually knows, it's a pain to extract enough if you're planning a party.

Electric domestic juicers, while excellent for nearly every other variety of fruit and vegetable, are problematic for citrus because if you juice with the skin on, you can be left with a distinct bitterness that can sometimes spoil a drink you subsequently mix. A quick solution can be to spend a moment peeling oranges or lemons before adding to a juicer.

With a domestic juicer, like the Sunbeam Juicer, it takes out the need for straining out blended fruit pulp. With the machine pulping, separating skins and seeds, and straining in one easy push of the button - Alakazam - instant juice and nectar. It's actually quite good fun!

fruit calendar

Although today we're lucky enough to get most fruits at any time of year, they're always at their best in season. Use this handy calendar to help you decide what to consider for your drinks menu. A drink like the Mango Motorhead (see page 112) made with tinned or imported mangoes just doesn't taste of summer the way one mixed with a ripe, juicy, fresh mango does!

The gradient represents the time which a particular fruit is in season or available in the fruit calendar.

fruit	summer	autumn	winter	spring
apple				
apricot				
banana				
grapes				
honeydew melon				
lemon				
mandarin				
mango				
orange				
passionfruit				
peach				
pear				
pineapple				
plum				
strawberries				

carrot soup juice

Carrot Soup juice? Yes, it does sound silly. But on our last night in Morocco, Esmeralda and I travelled to the picturesque little mountain village of Chefchaouen. All the houses were daub and wattle, painted blue and white, and by the time we'd threaded our way through thin Riff Mountains air and winding lanes to the most expensive hotel in town, we were starving.

The most luxurious room at the Hotel Asthma was the princely sum of $US 85.00. Suddenly feeling the cold, we decided to order the carrot soup. I'm not that familiar with Moroccan cuisine but somehow a bowl of grated carrot floating in chilled freshly juiced orange juice didn't seem quite so appetising - especially after we were given the bill for the outrageous sum of $US 5 per bowl.

Surprisingly, though, it was actually quite tasty - and as Esmeralda pointed out, it could've been worse - imagine hot freshly juiced orange juice!

Makes 2 drinks
2 decent sized carrots
2 large navel oranges
ice

Juice carrots and peeled oranges. Stir before pouring over ice in old-fashioned glasses. You might like to drink this through a straw as the carrot can stain your lips.

freshly whipped pineapple is nature's cappuccino

pineapple pleasure chest

Every morning, when my work team start the day, we like to share a fruit whip. And every morning, my good mate Bodhi likes to remind me that 'freshly whipped pineapple is nature's cappuccino. You can use that in one of your books if you like, Woody.' And so I have. And it is true: it does form a very foamy froth, just like a cappuccino!

Makes 2 drinks
¼ pineapple, peeled and cut into long strips
2 bananas, peeled
120ml / 4oz Lipton Flavoured Black Tea Vanilla, steeped and chilled
ice

Juice banana, followed by pineapple to flush the flavour of the banana through juicer. Stir with chilled tea before pouring over ice into highball glasses.

ginger energy blast

Makes 2 drinks
3cm / 1¼ inch knob of ginger, unpeeled
4 large navel oranges
ice

Juice ginger, followed by oranges to flush the flavour of the ginger through juicer. Stir before pouring over ice into old-fashioned glasses.

pretty peach apple

It can be pretty tricky to find peach nectar on its own in the supermarket. It's often sold in combination with other juices such as apple or mango. Peaches aren't a very juicy fruit and it is more expensive to juice them, given their stone - but they do work well with juicier fruit like apples.

Makes 1L, 2 pints or 4 drinks
2 peaches, pitted and peeled
1 whole red delicious apple, small
1 lemon, peeled
ice

Juice peaches first, followed by apple and lemon to flush through the flavour of the peach. Stir honey into juice before pouring over ice into old-fashioned glasses.

mango motorhead

Makes 2 drinks
1 large mango, pitted and peeled
1 large navel orange
1 punnet strawberries, pruned
ice

Juice all ingredients. Stir before pouring over ice into old-fashioned glasses.

gettin' juicy in the kitchen

passion bootie

If you want to impress then you don't have to buy big gifts, sports cars or diamond rings. Try the little sensitive things that'll make everyone shake their bootie. No alcohol here, just pure passion bootie pleasure.

Makes 2 drinks
3 mandarins, peeled
1 lime, peeled
1 small whole granny smith apple,
2 passionfruits, squeezed and stirred through
ice

Juice ingredients, excluding passionfruit and ice, into a small jug then stir through. Pour over ice in cocktail glasses, squeeze passionfruit through before serving.

passion pear zing

Makes 2 drinks
2 pears
1 lemon, peeled
1 small whole granny smith apple,
2 passionfruits, squeezed and stirred through
ice

Juice ingredients, excluding passionfruit and ice, into a small jug then stir through. Pour over ice in cocktail glasses, squeeze passionfruit through before serving.

celery crunch lunch

I love celery: raw, cooked or juiced. Any which way! By adding some fresh peppercorns, a couple of apples and a little parsley to the juicer, I get a lunch in a glass I can drink in a flash… And when it comes to crunch time, just add a little sea salt to the rim of the glass to finish.

Makes 4 drinks

6 celery stalks

2 granny smith apples, chopped

1 teaspoon fresh peppercorns

½ cup parsley

lime squeeze, to garnish

sea salt rim, to garnish (see p 25)

ice

Juice all ingredients except ice. Stir before pouring over ice into highball glasses. Garnish with sea salt rim and lime squeeze.

strawberry fair

Makes 2 drinks

1 peach, pitted

1 pear

½ lemon, peeled

1 punnet strawberries, pruned

ice

Juice all ingredients except ice. Stir before pouring over ice into old-fashioned glasses.

plum courage

Makes 2 drinks

6 large dark plums, pitted

1 large orange, peeled

6 strawberries, pruned

ice

Juice all ingredients except ice. Stir before pouring over ice into highball glasses. Garnish with plum slices.

melon hook

I could never understand why people would choose honeydew melons - or any fruit, for that matter! - over a rich, calorie-laden cake or pastry for dessert. But as my palate has matured, I've come to love the sweet, almost perfumed delicacy of honeydew melons and the way they interact with watermelon and fennel in this drink make it almost addictive.

Makes 4 drinks

½ honeydew melon

4 large wedges watermelon

2 teaspoons fennel seeds

ice

Juice fennel seeds first, followed by remaining ingredients. Stir before pouring over ice into wine glasses.

plum courage, melon hook

cool cucumber

Cool, crisp and always refreshing, cucumbers add a mellowness that offsets the crunchy tartness of the granny smith apples.

Makes 2 drinks

½ cucumber

1 cup fresh mint

2 small granny smith apples, whole

cucumber sliced, to garnish

ice

Juice mint first, followed by cucumber and apples to flush the flavours of the mint through juicer. Stir before pouring over ice into highball glasses. Garnish with a cucumber sliced lengthways.

plum, orange and strawberry juicy fruit

Makes 4 drinks

12 large dark red plums, pitted

2 large navel oranges

1 punnet strawberries, pruned

ice

Juice all ingredients except ice. Stir before pouring over ice into old-fashioned glasses.

tangy tango

I remember when the fruiterer first cut a Panamanian passionfruit open for me, to reveal a fruit with so much more to offer than the usual common varieties. They are slightly sweeter and creamier to taste. Growing as large as baseballs, easier to cut and with much more pulp, they don't dry up or become hard as quickly. However, if you can't get hold of Panamanian passionfruit, the standard variety will do just fine.

Makes 2 drinks
2 mangoes, pitted and peeled
¼ papaya, cut into wedges
1 lime, peeled
1 Panamanian passionfruit, halved; or 3 passionfruit, halved
ice

Juice ingredients except ice and passionfruit. Stir squeezed passionfruit pulp through juice before pouring over ice into highball glasses.

kiwi lemon lush

If you're setting up for a cocktail party and you've been preparing zest garnishes during the day - you'll have to try this.

Makes 2 drinks
2 lemons, peeled
4 kiwi fruit,
30ml / 1oz maple syrup
sparkling water, to top (optional)
kiwi fruit wedge, to garnish
ice

Juice all ingredients except ice and maple syrup. Stir maple syrup through juice before pouring over ice into highball glasses. Top with sparkling water for a sparkling effect. Garnish with kiwi wedge.

carrot cake in a glass

Although I love carrot cake, I've never been able to bake a good one. However, with a little experimentation, I was able to turn my favourite cake into a hip and groovy afternoon juice.

Makes 4 drinks
2 carrots
1 cup table grapes
4 apricots
1 cup sultanas
table grapes, to garnish
ice

Juice sultanas first, followed by apricots, grapes and carrots so as to flush the flavours of the less juicy ingredients through. Stir before pouring over ice into cocktail glasses.

back yard fruit juice

As a kid I remember having all four ingredients of the juice below growing in an orchard on our farm. I've learned since then that having the luxury of an orchard or simply the space to grow one is a rare one, especially in the city! For those who have small back yards (like me), the plants and trees that grow the ingredients below, flourish in decent sized pots. With potted fruit bearing plants, you'll turn your backyard into a mini orchard.

Makes 2 drinks
3 mandarins, peeled
1 lime, peeled
1 small whole granny smith apple,
2 passionfruit, squeezed and stirred through
ice

Juice all ingredients except passionfruit and ice. Stir passionfruit through before pouring over ice into old-fashioned glasses.

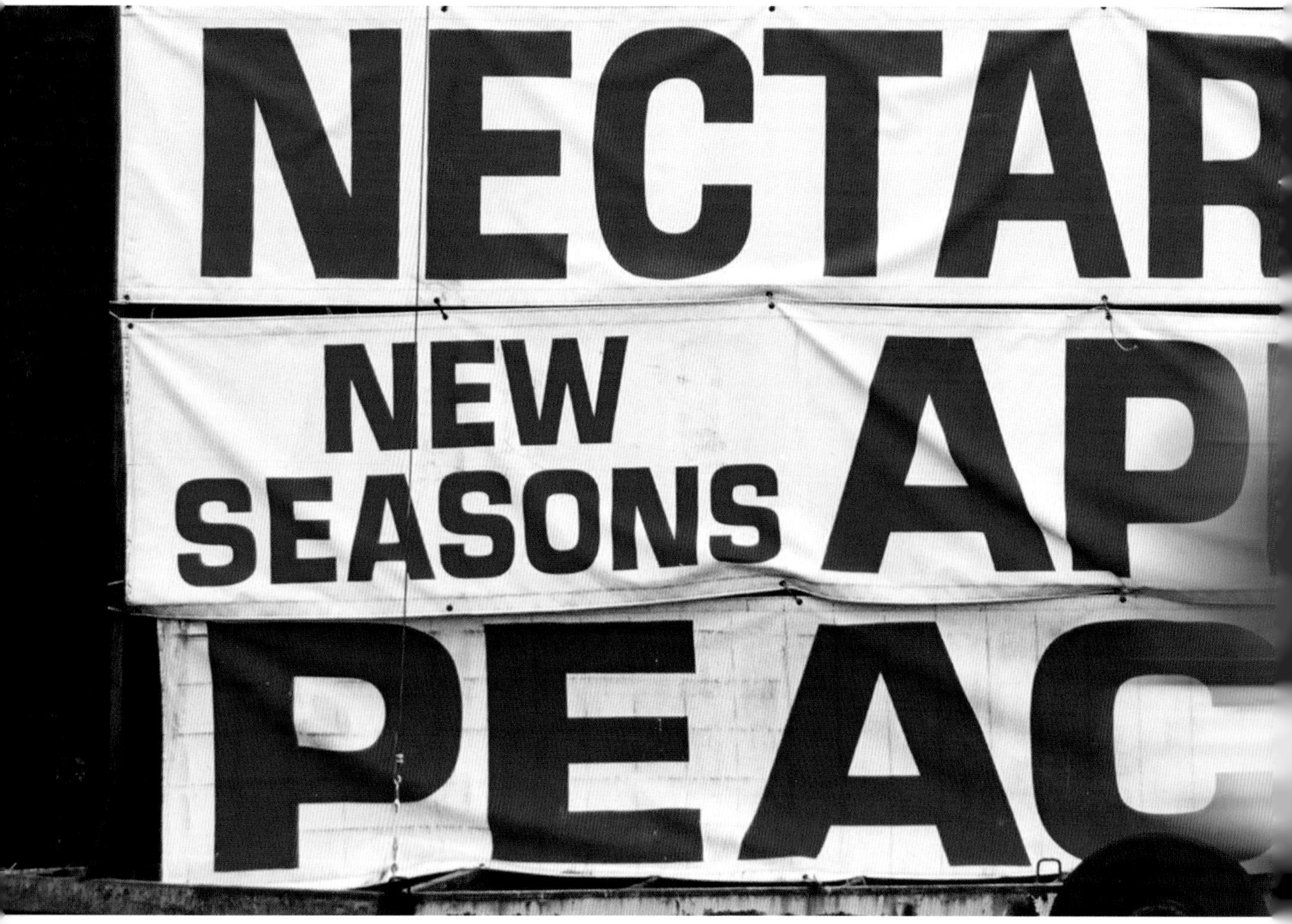
NECTAR
NEW
SEASONS

woody stocks up on fresh fruit

tea beet juice

Makes 4 drinks

2 beetroot, raw

3cm / 1¼ inch knob ginger

1 lime, peeled

200ml / 7oz Lipton Lemon Herbal Infusion, steeped and chilled

60ml / 2oz liquid honey

ice

Juice ingredients except ice and maple syrup. Stir liquid honey through juice before pouring over ice into highball glasses.

banana, pear and apple zapper

I once read a story in the newspaper about a villain who'd successfully robbed three banks with nothing more than a banana in his pocket. No, he wasn't just excited to be there. I always imagined the hapless teller being ribbed by their colleagues over being robbed by a banana-wielding bandit. And I wonder what kind of post-traumatic stress disorder they'd suffer if they walked past fruit shops…

Makes 4 drinks

4 bananas

2 pears, de-stalked

4 red delicious apples

ice

Juice bananas first, followed by pears and apples to flush flavours through juicer. Stir before pouring over ice into highball glasses.

herbie

Fresh herbs are really cool to add to the juicer, but remember to put them through first so the juice from the next ingredient can flush the flavours through the juicer.

Makes 4 drinks
½ cup fresh thyme or marjoram
½ cup fresh mint
½ cup fresh basil
4 kiwi fruit
2 limes
4 apples
ice

Juice herbs first, followed by remaining ingredients except ice. Stir before pouring over ice into shot glasses.

*This is a much more palatable hangover cure
than wheatgrass... or a raw egg!*

stoney fruit fix

Makes 2 drinks
4 apricots
4 plums
4 peaches
1 lime
ice

Juice all ingredients except ice. Stir before pouring over ice into old-fashioned glasses.

the blender

A good blender, like the Sunbeam Café Series blender, will keep all your blended drinks looking fresh and inviting.

Add the listed ingredients to a blender with ice equal to the capacity of the glass. Before blending make sure the lid is on and apply pressure to the blender cup to keep it on the motor base. Remove the cup and shake the ingredients before blending a second time to ensure all the ingredients are consistently mixed. The important thing here is to judge for yourself when the ingredients have been blended thoroughly.

tomato tosca

If you want a brekkie drink that jumps around in your mouth then try this. It jumps from sweet maple to savoury parsley, then from hot chilli to cold ice. Just like a frozen Bloody Mary, but without the alcohol. Like the Scorpion Sting on page 177, you can substitute the chilli for 2-3 fresh peppercorns and have a less spicing flavour. Dried whole peppercorns won't break down easily in a blender. You can also use cracked or ground pepper if you like.

Makes 1 drink
60ml / 2oz Ocean Spray Cranberry Classic juice
½ roma tomato, chopped
¼ lime, juiced
¼ jalapeño chilli, chopped
1 tablespoon parsley, chopped
20ml / ¾oz maple syrup
ice

Blend all ingredients with ice until smooth. Serve in chilled champagne saucer. Make sure you wash your hands carefully in cool water after handling chillis.

pepperhead

Using contrasting flavours such as mango and pepper in a drink not only provides a hot and cold sensation to dwell on in the mouth, the two also work well to match sweet and savoury in quite a harmonious way. Like French wine makers who add cracked pepper to bowls of vanilla ice cream before eating, Pepperhead is the avant-garde alcohol free blend of flavour. Try it with fresh peppercorns for a more perfumed flavour.

Makes 1 drink

30ml / 1oz Ocean Spray White Cranberry juice

30ml / 1oz freshly juiced orange juice

20ml / ¾oz liquid honey

¼ mango, peeled and pitted

1 teaspoon cracked pepper

1 fresh kaffir lime leaf, to garnish

ice

Blend all ingredients with ice until smooth. Serve in chilled highball glass. Garnish with fresh kaffir lime leaf.

mango ginger groove

Looking for a groovy drink to serve at brunch? Mango Ginger Groove will get you and your friends into a groove that'll keep them coming back for more. It is packed with sweet flavours of mango and banana, and bursting with the uplifting buzz of ginger. A nice alternative is to substitute mango for peach, plum or rock melon.

Makes 1 drink
60ml / 2oz Ocean Spray White Cranberry juice
¼ mango peeled and pitted
1 banana zested
2 teaspoons ginger, chopped
ice

Blend all ingredients until smooth. Serve in chilled highball glasses.

sour cherry chocolate buster

Makes 1 drink

30ml / 1oz Ocean Spray Ruby Red Grapefruit juice

30ml / 1oz lime juice

2-3 dashes Angostura bitters

5 fresh black cherries, pitted and stalks removed

30ml / 1oz chocolate topping

chocolate topping, to garnish

ice

Blend all ingredients until smooth. Serve in large chilled cocktail glass. Garnish with chocolate topping on inside of glass.

Chocolate topping can make a fun-looking garnish. Hold glass on a 45 degree angle and drizzle topping in while slowly turning stem of glass.

wake me up little ginger

Makes 1 drink

60ml / 2oz apricot nectar

½ peach, pitted

2 teaspoons chopped ginger

1 fresh kaffir lime leaf

ice

Blend all ingredients until smooth. Serve in highball glasses.

get set brekkie

All that's missing are the fried eggs, hash browns and a side of bacon. If you're in a rush then this is for you... better to gulp and go than gobble and go.

Makes 1 drink
60ml / 2oz mango nectar
60ml / 2oz freshly drawn espresso
60ml / 2oz milk
½ cup your favourite dried cereal
30ml maple syrup
ice

Blend all ingredients until smooth. Serve in highball glass.

apple turnover

Makes 1 drink
30ml / 1oz Ocean Spray White Cranberry juice
60ml / 2oz milk
½ cup your favourite dried cereal (I like oat-based fruit cereal best)
½ red delicious apple, cored and chopped
2 teaspoons caster sugar
ice

Blend all ingredients until smooth. Serve in highball glass.

You can use any of your favourite dried cereal.
I like oat-based fruit cereal best - and friends have used apple and cinnamon granola
to really apple-ise their turnover!

liqueurs and
infusions

One of the most amazing and inspiring experiences I've ever had was when I was lucky enough to be a part of The Great Barrier Feast on beautiful Hamilton Island, part of the Whitsundays group of tropical islands in the middle of the Great Barrier Reef. The Great Barrier Feast is one of the most exclusive and indulgent food festivals in Australia, if not the world, attracting over one hundred and fifty of the world's most committed gourmands for three days of feasting and celebrating.

Hamilton Island is almost a cliché: crystal clear water warm as a bath; golden beaches that go on forever; a lush and tropical setting which proved to be just perfect for chefs of the calibre of Stephanie Alexander and Curtis Stone to present seven-course banquets, all complemented by the finest Australian and international wines… and a few original cocktail creations by yours truly.

The drinks I'd prepared for guests' arrival went down a treat. Who can say no to a delicious Marmalade Margarita Punch (see page 96). The next day, a simple Sangria and my now famous Spiced Gypsy Punch (see page 98) were just as popular at an impressive tapas lunch.

I suppose being surrounded by so many amazing chefs and food and wine professionals preparing delicacies of indescribable delectability for such knowledgeable and discerning connoisseurs might be considered a little… well, intimidating. Having come from a busy city, not having had a day off in ten weeks, and preparing over 10,000 cocktails in a month might have been enough to ensure I might lose it - let alone that I only had forty minutes to prepare between the time my plane landed and serving the first 180 cocktails.

And yet, I was surprisingly chilled, like any good cocktail - or cocktail mixer! It probably had a lot to do with the beautiful surroundings, the wonderful food, and the relaxed vibe on the island. Although the pressure was on - given the number of cocktails to serve and the demanding discernment of the clientele, it was the fact that I'd planned and prepared my cocktails and infusions long before, that allowed me to enjoy myself as much as I did. And a great beach helps too!

infuse

You can impart the flavour of any desired fruit, spice or other ingredient to alcohol by simply simmering them with sugar over low heat. The longer the ingredients simmer the stronger the flavour will be - but at the expense of alcohol, which evaporates in heat. A little citric acid that can be picked up in almost every supermarket (check the spice and baking section), can help balance sweetness and add further complexity and depth. I use this to differentiate the liqueurs. Infused liqueurs are terribly easy to make, wonderfully delicious to drink and great fun to make. And they're perfect for easy, memorable gifts when presented in a special bottle.

hot infuse - method

Add all ingredients except alcohol-free liquids and half of alcohol to large saucepan. Warm ingredients and simmer over low heat for 20 minutes, ensuring not to boil. Stir occasionally.

Spices and nuts should be dry roasted first. This releases their natural oils and thereby increases their flavour intensity and character.

Remove from heat and add remaining ingredients as listed in recipe, stirring thoroughly. Once the infusion has cooled it can be strained and served straight away, but for a better result: leave covered in a cool place for 24-48 hours, stirring occasionally to break up sediment. Strain off solids using sieve.

toasted coconut liqueur

Makes 700ml / 23½oz or approximately 23 drinks
350ml / 12oz Remy Martin Grand Cru cognac
350ml / 12oz water
200g / 7oz coconut, desiccated
200g / 7oz sugar

In pot over medium heat, dry roast coconut for 5-8 minutes or until brown. Add sugar, water and half the cognac then simmer for 20 minutes over low heat. Remove from heat and strain off coconut. Add remaining cognac and stir. Cool for 30 minutes. Seal in sterilized bottles and store for up to 1 month in fridge. For more on bottle sterilization, see page 43.

tiramisu dark liqueur

Makes 700ml / 23½oz or approximately 23 drinks

350ml / 12oz Havana Club Añejo Blanco rum

100ml / 3½oz espresso coffee

250ml / 9oz water

100g / 3½oz cooking chocolate (80% cocoa)

200g / 7oz sugar

white chocolate curls, to garnish (see p 240)

Melt chocolate in pot over low heat. Add espresso, sugar (water or dairy depending on recipe) and half the rum and simmer for 20 minutes over low heat. Remove from heat then add remaining rum and stir. Cool for 30 minutes. Seal in sterilized bottles and store for up to 1 month in fridge. I've listed two recipes - one for those who like their tiramisu a little dark, and those who prefer something suitably rich. For more on hot infusions, see page 144; and for more on bottle sterilization, see page 43.

tiramisu crème liqueur

Every good patisserie will have tiramisu. A rich yet delicate combination of chocolate and espresso coffee, it's hard to resist. Like the ever-addictive cake from which it takes its name, you'll find yourself slurping your way to the bottom of the glass.

Makes 700ml / 23½oz or approximately 23 drinks

350ml / 12oz Havana Club Añejo Blanco rum

100ml / 3½oz espresso coffee

100ml / 3½oz condensed milk

150ml / 5oz cream

100g / 3½oz cooking chocolate (80% cocoa)

100g / 3½oz sugar

vanilla sugar, to garnish

Muddle, stir and strain into chilled martini glass. Garnish with vanilla sugar rim (see page 25). Vanilla sugar can usually be found in the baking aisle of your supermarket. Keep in fridge for up to two weeks.

woody whips up a pot of passionfruit, plum liqueur

dark forest liqueur

Makes 700ml / 23½oz or approximately 23 drinks

350ml / 12oz Remy Martin Grand Cru cognac

350ml / 12oz water

200g / 7oz mixed berries (blackberries, strawberries, boysenberries etc)

200g / 7oz sugar

1 teaspoon citric acid (optional)

1 raspberry speared, to garnish

Simmer in pot for 20 minutes over low heat, half the cognac, water, sugar and mixed berries. Remove from heat and strain off berries. Add remaining cognac and stir. Cool for 30 minutes. Garnish with speared raspberry. Seal in sterilized bottles and store for up to 1 month in fridge.

passionfruit, plum liqueur

I love the texture and flavour of rich dark plums. So shiny and gleaming to the eye and so soft and juicy to the bite. They hold their flavour well in the fridge and sweeten considerably during prolonged storage time. Over-ripe plums are good to use in this recipe, as the sweeter the fruit, the more flavoursome the end result will be. If fresh passionfruit are not available, it is acceptable to use tinned passionfruit in liqueurs due to cooking time. You should be able to find the tinned variety in most supermarkets.

Makes 700ml / 23½oz or approximately 23 drinks

350ml / 12oz Cuervo tequila

350ml / 12oz water

5 dark red dark plums, pitted and chopped

5 passionfruit, pulped and de-seeded; or ½ cup tinned passionfruit pulp, de-seeded

200g / 7oz palm sugar

lime wheel, to garnish

Simmer plums, passionfruit, water, sugar and half the tequila in pot for 20 minutes over low heat. Remove from heat and strain off fruit. Add remaining tequila and stir. Cool for 30 minutes. Garnish with lime wheel. Seal in sterilized bottles and store for up to 1 month in fridge. For more on hot infusion, see page 144; and for more on bottle sterilization, see page 43.

barley-buca liqueur

This is a great recipe for those who like the liquoricey taste of sambuca but shy away from its astonishingly high alcohol taste. Often associated with terribly drunken nights that people often wish they could forget, it's a nice change to appreciate the sharp flavour of aniseed without any subsequent hangovers or regrets.

Makes 700ml / 23½oz or approximately 23 drinks
350ml / 12oz Cuervo tequila
350ml / 12oz water
200g / 7oz barley sugar candies
2 tablespoons star anise, crushed
100g / 3½oz brown sugar

In pot over medium heat, dry roast star anise for 2 minutes or until brown. Add candy, sugar and half the tequila then simmer for 20 minutes over low heat. Remove from heat and strain off spice. Add remaining ingredients and stir. Cool for 30 minutes. Seal in sterilized bottles and store for up to 1 month in fridge. For more on hot infusion, see page 144; and for more on bottle sterilization, see page 43.

white chocolate, raspberry liqueur

Makes 700ml / 23½oz or approximately 23 drinks
350ml / 12oz Havana Club Añejo Blanco rum
350ml / 12oz full cream
100g / 3½oz white cooking chocolate
1 punnet or 100g / 3½oz fresh raspberries
100g / 3½oz sugar

This recipe requires two pots cooking at the same time. In first pot, simmer raspberries in half the rum over low heat for 20 minutes. Strain off raspberries. Add sugar and cream and stir over low heat for further 2 minutes.

In second pot, slowly melt white cooking chocolate over low heat. Once melted, gradually add rum, a little at a time, stirring thoroughly. Once sugar has dissolved in first pot, add strained contents to second pot. Combine thoroughly and cook over low heat for a further two minutes. Cool for 30 minutes. Seal in sterilized bottles and store for up to two weeks in fridge. For more on hot infusion, see page 144; and for more on bottle sterilization, see page 43.

White cooking chocolate can usually be bought in a block or in buttons by the packet. Look in the baking aisle of your supermarket.

mango, cardamom liqueur

Makes 700ml / 23½oz or approximately 23 drinks
240ml / 8oz Havana Club Añejo Blanco rum
120ml / 4oz Midori
350ml / 12oz mango nectar
5 cardamom pods, crushed
200g / 7oz palm sugar, broken into 1cm chunks

In pot over medium heat, dry roast cardamom for 2 minutes or until brown. Add mango nectar, sugar and rum, then simmer for 20 minutes over low heat. Remove from heat and strain off fruit. Add remaining ingredients and stir. Cool for 30 minutes. Seal in sterilized bottles and store for up to 1 month in fridge.

cinnamon, pear liqueur, strawberry liqueur, ginger liqueur

cinnamon pear liqueur

Makes 700ml / 23½oz or approximately 23 drinks

350ml / 12oz 42 Below vodka

350ml / 12oz water

2 pears, cored and chopped

2 cinnamon quills

1 teaspoon citric acid

200g / 7oz sugar

Simmer water, pears, cinnamon quills, citric acid, sugar and half the vodka in pot for 20 minutes over low heat. Remove from heat and strain off pears. Add remaining vodka and stir. Cool for 30 minutes. Seal in sterilized bottles and store for up to 1 month in fridge. For more on hot infusion, see page 144; and for more on bottle sterilization, see page 43.

strawberry liqueur

Makes 700ml / 23½oz or approximately 23 drinks

350ml / 12oz 42 Below vodka

350ml / 12oz water

10 large strawberries, pruned and chopped

1 teaspoon citric acid

200g / 7oz sugar

Simmer water, strawberries, citric acid, sugar and half the vodka in pot for 20 minutes over low heat. Remove from the heat and strain off fruit. Add remaining vodka and stir. Cool for 30 minutes. Seal in sterilized bottles and store for up to 1 month in fridge. For more on hot infusion, see page 144; and for more on bottle sterilization, see page 43.

ginger liqueur

Makes 700ml / 23½oz or approximately 23 drinks

350ml / 12oz 42 Below vodka

350ml / 12oz water

100g / 3½oz ginger, chopped

200g / 7oz sugar

Simmer water, ginger, sugar and half the vodka in pot for 20 minutes over low heat. Remove from heat and strain off ginger. Add remaining vodka and stir. Cool for 30 minutes. Seal in sterilized bottles and store for up to 1 month in fridge. For more on hot infusion, see page 144; and for more on bottle sterilization, see page 43.

sour apple liqueur

Makes 700ml / 23½oz or approximately 23 drinks

350ml / 12oz 42 Below vodka

350ml / 12oz water

3 granny smith apples, peeled and chopped

2 teaspoons citric acid

200g / 7oz sugar

Simmer water, apples, citric acid, sugar and half the vodka in pot for 20 minutes over low heat. Remove from heat and strain off apples. Add remaining vodka and stir. Cool for 30 minutes. Seal in sterilized bottles and store for up to 1 month in fridge. For more on hot infusion, see page 144; and for more on bottle sterilization, see page 43.

watermelon, mango liqueur

Makes 700ml / 23½oz or approximately 23 drinks

350ml / 12oz 42 Below vodka

350ml / 12oz water

2 bags Lipton Green Tea with Mango

2 bags Lipton Watermelon Herbal Infusion

1 teaspoon citric acid (optional)

200g / 7oz sugar

Simmer water, tea bags, citric acid, sugar and half the vodka in pot for 20 minutes over low heat. Remove from heat and remove tea bags. Add remaining vodka and stir. Cool for 30 minutes. Seal in sterilized bottles and store for up to 1 month in fridge. For more on hot infusion, see page 144; and for more on bottle sterilization, see page 43.

lemon lux liqueur

Makes 700ml / 23½oz or approximately 23 drinks

350ml / 12oz Remy Martin Grand Cru cognac

350ml / 12oz water

2 bags Lipton Lemon Herbal Infusion

zest of 2 lemons

200g / 7oz sugar

Simmer water, lemon zest, herbal infusion bags, sugar and half the cognac in pot for 20 minutes over low heat. Remove from heat and strain off zest and bags. Add remaining cognac and stir. Cool for 30 minutes. Seal in sterilized bottles and store for up to 1 month in fridge. For more on hot infusion, see page 144; and for more on bottle sterilization, see page 43.

pecan pear crème liqueur

I once enjoyed the most amazing pastry when I was in France. It's said the magic is in the hands of the patissier and the spell is cast on the patron's mouth. Light and flaky pastry with a rich yet subtle butteriness, complemented the wonderful pecan fondant inside. What a treasure!

Pecans can be substituted for any other meaty dark nut: walnuts, hazelnuts or brazil nuts. Whichever you use, however, if they aren't blanched (their skins removed), you'll need to use a fine sieve to strain the husks. A liqueur should be as smooth and delicate as a fine French pastry, not lumpy with the remnants of solid ingredients.

Makes 700ml / 23½oz or approximately 23 drinks
350ml / 12oz Grand Marnier
150ml / 5oz milk
150ml / 5oz full cream
100g / 3½oz pecan nuts, crushed
2 pears, chopped
200g / 7oz sugar

In pot over medium heat, dry roast pecans for 2 minutes or until brown. Add pears, sugar, milk and cream and half the Grand Marnier then simmer for 20 minutes over low heat. Remove from heat and strain off fruit and nuts. Add remaining liqueur and stir. Cool for 30 minutes. Seal in sterilized bottles and store for up to two weeks in fridge. For more on hot infusion, see page 144; and for more on bottle sterilization, see page 43.

cold infused vodkas

A cold infusion of vodka with other ingredients imparts a subtle flavour and aroma that intensifies with time. Almost like wine, the flavour grows in depth and character over a few weeks before its inevitable decline. Cold infusions are best kept in the fridge or freezer and last for 1 month before ingredients begin to break down.

Experimenting with different ingredients and the flavours they impart is an imaginative way to lend your cocktails a new twist. I like to use slightly different and unexpected ingredients like cucumber or basil; the cucumber softens the spirit while basil adds perfume.

It's an especially good alternative to the traditional, straight-up martini. Try infusing vodka with interesting combinations such as: cucumber, basil, chilli, saffron and orange zest, lemongrass or a combination like strawberry, fresh kaffir lime and vanilla.

I prefer to use a pure, premium vodka like 42 Below for cold infusions. The infusion of ingredients in a neutral spirit imparts a more clean and distinct flavour. Having said that, rum would be my next option if I had to choose a substitute. I have tried some infused Mauritian rums before and although they're stronger to taste than vodka, they're still worth trying for something different. If you'd prefer something smoother, why not try a sweet, pure rum like Havana Club Añejo Blanco rum?

Try an infused vodka for a new and exciting variation on any of the vodka based martini recipes in the Sexy Martinis chapter (see page 170 for more). With a little experimentation and patience, you could turn any crazy or unusual combination into an exciting new cocktail creation!

cold infuse - method

Remove (or drink!) approximately 90ml / 3oz of spirit from bottle. Add ingredients and reseal bottle. Leave for at least 4 days before drinking.

Cold infused spirits are best served chilled or frozen and often as a shot or in martini-style cocktails to best showcase their flavours.

cucumber vodka

Makes 700ml
610ml / 10oz 42 Below vodka
1 cucumber sliced lengthways

Slice cucumber lengthways and add to bottle of vodka. Reseal and leave to infuse for 4 days. Keep refrigerated. Serve chilled.

chilli vodka

Makes 700ml
610ml / 10oz 42 Below vodka
4-6 chillis, sliced lengthways

Put a slice lengthways in chillis and add to bottle of vodka. Reseal and leave to infuse for 4 days. Keep refrigerated. Serve chilled.

saffron and orange vodka

Makes 700ml
610ml / 10oz 42 Below vodka
zest of 1 orange
8 strands of saffron

Add ingredients to bottle of vodka. Reseal and leave to infuse for 4 days. Keep refrigerated. Serve chilled.

infused vodkas are always impressive not to mention tasty

basil vodka

Makes 700ml

610ml / 20oz 42 Below vodka

15 basil leaves, ripped or bruised

Rip or bruise basil leaves slightly and add to bottle of vodka. Reseal and leave to infuse for 4 days. Keep refrigerated. Serve chilled.

kaffir, strawberry and vanilla vodka

Makes 700ml

610ml / 20oz 42 Below vodka

10 kaffir leaves, ripped or bruised

1 punnet strawberries, pruned and sliced

1 vanilla bean, split and scored

Put all ingredients into bottle of vodka. Reseal and leave to infuse for 4 days. Keep refrigerated. Serve chilled.

caramelized hazelnut and lemongrass vodka

Makes 700ml

610ml / 20oz 42 Below vodka

100g / 3½oz hazelnuts

3 lemongrass stems, split

½ cup brown sugar

90ml / 3oz water

Caramelize hazelnuts and sugar in pot with water until sticky. Add hazelnuts and lemongrass to bottle of vodka. Reseal and leave to infuse for 4 days. Keep refrigerated. Serve chilled.

kaffir, vanilla and pear vodka

Makes 700ml

610ml / 20oz 42 Below vodka

15 kaffir leaves, ripped or bruised

1 pear, cored and sliced

Put all ingredients into bottle of vodka. Reseal and leave to infuse for 4 days. Keep refrigerated. Serve chilled.

anise and manuka vodka

Makes 700ml

610ml / 20oz 42 Below Manuka vodka

10 star anise

Dry roast star anise in pot for 2 minutes. Add to bottle of vodka. Reseal and leave to infuse for 4 days. Keep refrigerated. Serve chilled.

cashew and sultana vodka

Makes 700ml

610ml / 20oz 42 Below vodka

60g / 2oz cashew nuts, unsalted

30g / 1oz sultanas

Dry roast cashew nuts in pot. Add cashews and sultanas to bottle of vodka. Reseal and leave to infuse for 4 days. Keep refrigerated. Serve chilled.

sexy martinis

One of the most outrageous celebrities I've had at my bar would be Quentin Tarantino. Just like his movies, he's funny, hyperactive and a little crazy. It was the launch of his much-awaited magnum opus, Kill Bill Volume One, and anyone who was someone - and anyone who wanted to be someone - was at a secret location for 300 guests in Sydney's Chinatown... well, as secret as it could be, given that it somehow managed to fill to a capacity of over 500 people.

In the middle of the party, was a life-size ice sculpture of one of the characters from the film, the wizened kung-fu master Pai Mei played by the renowned Hong Kong action star Gordon Liu. It was carved by the world champion ice sculptor Kengi, whose art has been passed down from father to son for generations... a third generation ice sculpture master, he still uses his grandfather's heirloom knives to carve life from massive blocks of solid ice.

As the night wore on, my specially-commissioned Tarantino martinis slid down like ninjas on silk sheets. It was getting seriously crazy! The star of the night responded by acting out a scene from the movie. Flamboyantly and enthusiastically grabbing Kengi's heirloom sword, he attacked the sculpture, hacking off a hand, then an arm. The crowd screamed for more. No mean swordsman himself, Quentin went for Pai Mei's head, and with the tenth blow, he at last lopped it clean off.

Smashing, bashing, grunting and gurning, he finally managed to send the whole sculpture tumbling into a thousand chilly shards with a decisive blow to the waist. It wasn't pretty to watch, but we all loved it. Well, almost all of us. For with that final lunge, he also managed to break Kengi's grandfather's sword.

It almost seemed like a scene from one of his movies; suddenly the air was charged by the possibility of a stand-off between Pi Mie's creator and destroyer. But after another visit to the bar, a couple more Tarantino martinis, an apology and some restitution, all was forgiven.

Woody says: Grasshopper, alcohol and ice sculpture swords do not always mix.

The martini is the king of cocktails, so simple and yet so important to make properly - let alone do well! And yet, it's also one of the most adaptable cocktails, with traditional variations such as the vodka martini (or vodkatini, James Bond's poison of choice); the Gibson (with garlic and a cocktail onion); the manhattan (using bourbon and sweet and dry vermouth) and the Tequini (using tequila) appealing to every taste. In this chapter, we'll also look at newer varieties, including the rikki (a shorter, sharper martini-style drink) and, of course, the infamous Tarantino martini, which you can find on p 173.

Some of the martini recipes, and other drink recipes for that matter, include the addition of chilled flavoured tea. Here is a basic method to enable the use of a refreshing and inexpensive ingredient in your drinks and cocktails. For more on iced tea, see page 298 in the Take the Plunge chapter.

classic dry martini

Martinis are the cocktail equivalent of the classic white shirt or little black dress. They're an indispensable part of drinking culture, and while fashions may change, the martini never goes out of style.

The most iconic of all cocktails, the Martini has its own glass, its own brand of vermouth and even its own hour - the martini hour (usually sometime around five pm). Countless books and songs have been devoted to it and its pleasures. Why so much fuss about such a simple drink? After all, it's just gin or vodka and vermouth in a glass with an olive, isn't it?

As you'll see below, there are endless variations on this greatest of cocktails, and it's due in part to its simplicity. You cannot fudge the details with a Martini; you must use the best possible ingredients, as there's nowhere for the flaws to hide. Use a cheap base spirit, and you'll taste it. Use a quality vodka like 42 Below or an excellent gin like South, and you'll find the drink singing exultantly.

The whole process of Martini making - the chilling of glasses, shaking versus stirring, the garnish - have been subject to arcane ritual and endless debate. Much like the Japanese tea ceremony, it's as much the making of a Martini that's important as the drinking. However you make it, enjoy the process of mixing this most sophisticated, enduring drink. And enjoy!

classic dry martini - method

Makes 1 drink
90ml / 3oz South Gin or 42 Below Vodka
5-10ml / ¼oz dry vermouth
speared spanish olive, to garnish
ice

Depending on your taste, either stir and strain or shake and strain into a chilled martini glass. Garnish with speared Spanish olive. See page 30 and 33 for more on stirring and straining or shaking and straining.

An option with vermouth is to pour over ice while chilling glass and discard with ice so the flavour is very subtle. According to Winston Churchill, all that was needed was the shadow of the bottle to pass over the drink to make it suitably extra dry. The less vermouth added - the dryer the cocktail. And in yet another variation, vermouth can also be added to the mixing glass and stirred in with the gin or vodka. It's up to you!

tarantino martini

Makes 1 drink
30ml / 1oz 42 Below vodka
30ml / 1oz Midori
60ml / 2oz apple juice
30ml / 1oz maple syrup
long lemon rind, to garnish (see p 26)
ice

Shake and strain ingredients into a chilled martini glass. Garnish with long lemon rind. See page 30 for more on shaking and straining.

martini montana

Makes 1 drink
60ml / 2oz South gin
90ml / 3oz Ocean Spray Cranberry Blackcurrant juice
6 raspberries
1 lime wedge
1 vanilla bean, split, to garnish
ice

Muddle fruit in base of mixing glass then add remaining ingredients. Shake and double-strain into a chilled martini glass. Garnish with a split vanilla bean. See pages 30 and 33 for more on muddling, shaking and double-straining.

banjo martini

Makes 1 drink
45ml / 1¼oz 42 Below vodka
15ml / ½oz dry sherry
10 pomegranate seeds (to sink)
60ml / 2oz Ocean Spray White Cranberry Peach juice
lime rind, to garnish (see p 26)
ice

Shake and strain all ingredients over pomegranate seeds in base of a chilled martini glass. Garnish with lime rind. See page 30 for more on shaking and straining.

Lime rind is usually produced using a rind-cutting tool that cuts a thin, even strip of rind. By turning the fruit while firmly pressing the tool against the skin a long strip of skin is cut (rind is a long thin strip of citrus skin as opposed to zest, which is a shorter wider strip of citrus skin). If you don't have a rind-cutting tool, you can peel a large piece of skin with a paring knife , and then cut the skin into thin strips while placed flat on a cutting board.

scorpion sting

Even a quarter of a jalapeño chilli can be too much for some people. If you or your guests are sensitive to chilli, consider substituting cracked pepper instead.

Makes 1 drink
45ml / 1¼oz Midori
15ml / ½oz Cuervo tequila
60ml / 2oz Ocean Spray Cranberry Classic juice
1 lime wedge
¼ jalapeño chilli, chopped
3 teaspoons caster sugar
jalapeño chilli, sliced and de-seeded, to garnish
ice

Muddle fruit in base of mixing glass then add remaining ingredients. Shake and double-strain into a chilled martini glass. Garnish with a sliced chilli, being careful to remove seeds. A good idea is to make sure you wash your hands thoroughly after you handle chilli. See pages 30 and 33 for more on muddling, shaking and double-straining.

zagalia martini

Makes 1 drink
30ml / 1oz Havana Club Añejo Blanco rum
30ml / 1oz Grand Marnier
60ml / 2oz Lipton Flavoured Black Tea Hazelnut , steeped then chilled
1 lime wedge
1 dark plum, pitted
1 teaspoon caster sugar
fresh kaffir lime leaf, to garnish
ice

Muddle fruit in base of mixing glass then add remaining ingredients. Shake and double-strain into a chilled cocktail glass. Garnish with fresh kaffir lime leaf.

vanilla, rose martini, balino

vanilla, rose martini

When adding rose water to a drink, be judicious. A little too much can be way too much, overpowering the drink - and the unfortunate drinker! But here you'll find a little rose water works beautifully with grapefruit juice, making a floral and piquant cocktail with only a little sweetness.

Makes 1 drink
60ml / 2oz 42 Below vodka
60ml / 2oz Ocean Spray Ruby Red Grapefruit juice
3-4 dashes Angostura bitters
15ml / ½oz sugar syrup (see p 21)
5ml ¼oz rose water
½ vanilla bean, split and scored
rose petal, to garnish
ice

Shake and strain into a chilled martini glass. Garnish with rose petal. See pages 30 and 33 for more on shaking and straining.

balino

Makes 1 drink
30ml / 1oz Grand Marnier
30ml / 1oz Midori
90ml / 3oz Lipton Flavoured Black Tea Caramel, steeped then chilled
3 teaspoons lemongrass, chopped
skewered lemongrass, to garnish (see p 39)
ice

Muddle lemongrass with tea in base of mixing glass, then add remaining ingredients. Shake and strain into a chilled martini glass. Garnish with skewered lemongrass. See pages 30 and 33 for more on muddling, shaking and straining.

crisp apple chiquita

If you're looking for a cocktail to get people chatting, then this is a real tastebud tingler. Crisp fresh apple mixed with hot spicy ginger is a delicious flavour combination. When enriched with a little sugar and white cranberry juice, and boosted up with a good rum like Havana Club, the whole drink dances around like Chiquita stomping out a little flamenco rhythm on your tongue.

Makes 1 drink
60ml / 2oz Havana Club Añejo Blanco rum
60ml / 2oz Ocean Spray White Cranberry juice
¼ Granny Smith apple, cored and chopped
1 lime wedge
1 teaspoon ginger, chopped
1 teaspoon caster sugar
skewered apple fan, to garnish (see p 39)
ice

Muddle fruit in base of mixing glass then add remaining ingredients. Shake and double-strain into a chilled martini glass. Garnish with skewered apple fan. See pages 30 and 33 for more on muddling, shaking and double-straining.

mandarin meringue martini

I love the simplicity of using ingredients like ice cream. Almost every household has a tub. This is a base recipe for any combination of Grand Marnier, vodka, ice cream and fruit. You can try chocolate and orange, hazelnut and peach - or even caramel with tamarillo. Just follow the recipe but substitute the ingredients. You'll only be limited by your imagination!

Makes 1 drink
30ml / 1oz Grand Marnier
30ml / 1oz 42 Below vodka
2 teaspoons vanilla ice cream
½ mandarin, chopped, skin left on
1 teaspoon sugar
chocolate drops, to garnish (see below)
ice

Muddle mandarin with sugar in base of mixing glass then add remaining ingredients. Shake and double-strain into a chilled martini glass. Garnish with three chocolate drops. See pages 30 and 33 for more on muddling, shaking and double-straining.

To stick chocolate drops to the inside of glass, press drop against your thumb to melt a thin film of chocolate. Ensuring glass is cool and dry, press chocolate drops against it until set, usually within three seconds. This garnish also looks very good with the drops stuck to the outside of the glass.

apple groove tequini

Makes 1 drink

60ml / 2oz Cuervo tequila

30ml / 1oz Ocean Spray White Cranberry juice

4-5 dashes Angostura bitters

20ml / ¾oz sugar syrup (see p 21)

½ fuji apple, cored and chopped

1 teaspoon caster sugar

orange rind, to garnish (see p 26)

ice

Muddle apple and sugar syrup in base of mixing glass. Add remaining ingredients then shake and strain into a chilled martini glass. Garnish with orange rind. See pages 30 and 33 for more on muddling, shaking and straining.

caramel martini

Makes 1 drink

60ml / 2oz South gin

60ml / 2oz Lipton Flavoured Black Tea Caramel, steeped then chilled

30ml / 1oz maple syrup

ice

Shake and strain all ingredients. Pour into a chilled martini glass. See page 30 for more on shaking and straining.

zabaglione zone

It's a hard drink to pass. It tastes so good with the vanilla. The richness of the cognac and Grand Marnier makes this sweet and decadent cocktail a must for all sweet-toothed martini lovers.

Makes 1 drink
30ml / 1oz Grand Marnier
30ml / 1oz Remy Martin Grand Cru cognac
30ml / 1oz Ocean Spray White Cranberry juice
30ml / 1oz sweetened condensed milk
½ vanilla bean, split and scraped
cocoa dusting, to garnish
ice

Shake and strain into a chilled martini glass. Garnish with cocoa dusting. See page 30 for more on shaking and straining.

Cocoa dusting offers best results when ½ teaspoon of cocoa is placed in a sieve and then sprinkled over the drink. Using a small fine meshed sieve is convenient, but not essential. See page 36 for more on dusting.

soho

Makes 1 drink

60ml / 2oz 42 Below Manuka Honey vodka

30ml / 1oz Ocean Spray White Cranberry juice

15ml / ½oz lime juice

½ plum, chopped

½ pear, chopped

2 teaspoons caster sugar

skewered pear slice, to garnish (see p 39)

ice

Shake all ingredients in an ice-filled cocktail shaker. Strain and pour into a chilled cocktail glass. Garnish with skewered pear slice. See page 30 for more on shaking and straining.

grand apple tequini

Makes 1 drink

30ml / 1oz Cuervo tequila

30ml / 1oz Grand Marnier

30ml / 1oz sugar syrup (see p 21)

½ granny smith apple, cored and chopped

½ fresh lime, chopped

skewered apple fan, to garnish (see p 39)

ice

Muddle apple, lime and sugar syrup in base of mixing glass. Add remaining ingredients then shake and double strain into a chilled martini glass. Garnish with skewered apple fan. See pages 30 and 33 for more on muddling, shaking and double straining.

espressotini

I invited Paul Bassett, the World Champion Barista in 2004, to help me with my coffee skills. He makes some of the world's best coffee - and after a little presentation on how to work a home coffee machine, he made an artwork of coffee in my kitchen. This crazy combo of cocktail and coffee resulted in this version of the espressotini. Best of all, I got to drink it afterwards while he cleaned up the kitchen. A funny lesson learned - never judge a barista by the mess they make, but by the thoroughness of the clean - and the coffee. Needless to say Paul makes world-class coffee and leaves a once coffee-destroyed kitchen spotless.

Makes 1 drink

60ml / 2oz 42 Below vodka

30ml / 1oz Ocean Spray White Cranberry juice

30ml / 1oz espresso, chilled

2 teaspoons caster sugar

vanilla-flavoured sugar rim, to garnish (see below)

ice

Stir espresso with sugar in mixing glass and strain into a chilled martini glass. Layer chilled vodka and cranberry over espresso. The vodka cranberry mix can be stirred in the cocktail shaker instead of the mixing glass. Garnish with vanilla-flavoured sugar rim . For more on rimming, stirring and straining see pages 25 and 33.

To make the vanilla-flavoured sugar, mix 250g / 8oz caster sugar with one vanilla bean split and scraped and then mix together.

For those who don't have the luxury of a home espresso coffee machine, you might try instant coffee for an instant result. The flavour isn't quite as strong but a similar drink can be made…what would you call it? An Instantini?

stingray

Makes 1 drink

60ml / 2oz Cuervo tequila

30ml / 1oz Lipton Lemon Herbal Infusion, steeped and chilled

½ pear, cored and chopped

¼ jalapeño chilli (use ½ teaspoon pepper corns for less hot effect)

20ml / ¾oz sugar syrup (see p 21)

1 teaspoon caster sugar

pear slice, to garnish

ice

Muddle pear, chilli and sugar syrup in base of mixing glass. Add remaining ingredients then shake and strain into a chilled martini glass. Garnish with a pear slice. See page 30 for more on muddling, shaking and straining. You may opt to double-strain this cocktail so you don't get any surprise chilli seeds in your glass.

jasmine and vanilla martini

Dissecting a vanilla bean can be a little tricky. It's best to use a small sharp knife and while firmly pinning down the 'stalk' end of the bean with your fingers to the cutting board. Run a paring knife down lengthways to halve the bean. Then, using the flat of the knife blade, press down to open the split bean. Scrape the seeds out and add them to the shaker. Remember to always cut away from your fingers.

Makes 1 drink

60ml / 2oz 42 Below vodka or South gin

60ml / 2oz Lipton Green Tea with Jasmine, steeped and chilled

¼ vanilla bean, split and scraped

30ml / 1oz maple syrup

split vanilla bean, to garnish

ice

Shake and strain all ingredients into a chilled martini glass. Garnish with split vanilla bean. See pages 30 and 33 for more on shaking and double-straining.

dancing rikki

rikkis

Rikkis are my favourite afternoon pick-me-up should the occasion dictate a small celebration. The difference between a martini style drink and a rikki is that rikkis are smaller and sharper drinks, served in small glasses. The organised drinker will have, by way of natural instinct, all the ingredients and glassware stored in a convenient place in the freezer. The instant the moment arises, a rikki can be whipped up and put away within three minutes. Wham bam thank you rikki.

dancing rikki

Makes 1 drink
30ml / 1oz South gin
30ml / 1oz peach schnapps
1 cherry, speared, to garnish
ice

Pour ingredients straight from freezer into glass. Alternately, stir and strain into a chilled liqueur glass. Garnish with speared cherry. For more on stirring and straining, see page 33.

angel rikki

Makes 1 drink
30ml / 1oz white crème de cacao
30ml / 1oz framboise
1 fresh kaffir lime leaf, to garnish
ice

Pour ingredients straight from freezer into glass. Alternately, stir and strain into a chilled liqueur glass. Garnish with fresh kaffir lime leaf. For more on stirring and straining, see page 33.

perfect stranger

White crème de cacao is a clear white chocolate liqueur made with essence of cocoa. You can find it at most liquor stores but if you can't get any, try looking in the supermarket baking aisle for cocoa essence (not coconut essence with which it's sometimes confused). The replacement will mean you'll need to add 3-4 drops of essence to 30ml / 1oz of sugar syrup. For more on sugar syrup see page 21.

Makes 1 drink
30ml / 1oz Havana Club Añejo Blanco rum
30ml / 1oz white crème de cacao
60ml / 2oz Ocean Spray White Cranberry juice
1 chocolate mint stick, to garnish
ice

Stir and strain into a chilled martini glass. Garnish with chocolate mint stick. This garnish is simple and easy to find in most supermarkets. Sometimes purchased garnishes can make light work of garnish preparation.

fu manchu

Although I specify particular glasses with almost every drink, they're not obligatory. So you can feel comfortable about mixing a martini into any other glass other than a martini glass, I've made the recipe below for a split cocktail glass. Fu Manchu is very simple and very clean-flavoured. Sometimes just a few interesting flavours are all you need. So good, it's almost criminal!

Makes 1 drink
60ml / 2oz Cuervo tequila
30ml / 1oz liquid honey
60ml / 2oz Lipton Green Ice Tea
3 lemongrass stalks, 10cm lengths
ice

Shake and strain into a chilled cocktail glass. Garnish with lemongrass. For more on shaking and straining, see page 30.

perfume martini

Makes 1 drink

30ml / 1oz 42 Below vodka

30ml / 1oz white crème de cacao

60ml / 2oz Ocean Spray White Cranberry juice

30ml / 1oz sugar syrup (see p 21)

½ orange, zested

4 cloves

1 clove-studded orange zest, to garnish

ice

Muddle orange zest, cloves and sugar syrup in base of mixing glass. Add remaining ingredients then shake and double strain into a chilled martini glass. Garnish with clove-studded orange zest, made by cutting a thick piece of zest with a paring knife, and studding cloves in regular intervals on the rind side of zest. See page 26 for more on curling zest.

buster tequini

Makes 1 drink

60ml / 2oz Cuervo tequila

60ml / 2oz Ocean Spray Ruby Red Grapefruit juice

½ lime, chopped

1 cinnamon quill, broken in half

20ml / ¾oz sugar syrup (see p 21)

1 teaspoon sugar

1 cinnamon quill, to garnish

chocolate topping, to garnish

ice

Muddle lime and cinnamon with sugar syrup in base of mixing glass. Add remaining ingredients then shake and strain into a chilled martini glass. Garnish with cinnamon quill.

entrée and dessert cocktails

I'm not a big gambler - at least where casinos are concerned. To be honest, all those flashing lights and relentless bells and whistles make me crave the sanctuary of a dark bar with funky music and great cocktails.

So I can't quite explain how I found myself in the grand casino in St Malo, still dressed in my finest (or cleanest) backpacker clothes and still a little high on all the cheap booze I'd bought in the notorious tax haven of Bergerac. Okay, maybe that explains why I was there…

Anyway, despite looking awfully suspect in jeans and hiking boots, surrounded by sniffy Eurotrash in Jean-Paul Gaultier tuxes and dripping in Lacroix and bling, I cashed up with a couple of grands' worth of chips to try my luck at the roulette table.

Unlike it's poorer and flashier cousin in Vegas, French roulette is played with a big red ball on a much larger wheel. As I said before, I'm not a big gambler, and completely clueless, I ordered a glass of champagne and placed my bet. The wheel spins and before I realise what's happened… I win. So I'm a little up on the drinks tab and take another punt. And another. And another…

It must have been beginner's luck but in no time, the chips started piling up and I'd more than paid for my drinks - and more! My luck didn't run out that night, and neither did the champagne! I walked out 180,000 francs and quite a few bottles of champagne later, immediately removing myself from the soggy, overcrowded camping ground I was staying to more salubrious quarters in an impressive and luxurious old hotel on the hill overlooking the Casino.

After a week of total indulgence, working my way through a case of fine champagne and all the wonderful French food I could eat, I came up with the idea of mixing drinks with the local and very good bubbly. While I've never gambled again like I did that night, I'm glad to have gambled a little on experimenting with different flavours and food inspirations.

I find much of the inspiration for my own aperitif and digestif cocktails in memories of wonderful meals in world-renowned and dazzlingly inventive restaurants like Mezzo or Fat Duck in London; El Bulli in Barcelona; Sun Bar in Brisbane; or Wildfire in Sydney; and from the vast library of brilliant cookbooks we have at home, including the expansive Culinaria range of books.

Dessert cocktails are the perfect substitutes for cooking up chocolate pudding or spending hours baking cakes. They're decadent by nature, delicious in flavour and often induce naughty behaviour as a result. While I'm happy to take credit where credit's due for the recipes - I can't take any responsibility for what happens afterwards!

entrée cocktails - dry or perhaps a little sweet

The purpose of pre-dinner or aperitif cocktail is to excite the appetite and although they shouldn't be drunk with the meal, they're still important in creating a sense of expectation.

They've been very popular in the cafés, bars and restaurants of Europe for generations, especially between 5pm and 10pm (some Europeans, especially the Spanish, like to eat dinner late). As European palates are much drier than American or Australian tastes, I've slightly altered some of these aperitif-style drinks for sweeter toothed swillers. However, they can be made drier or less sweet by adding less sugar or more dry ingredients.

chandelier

With so much recent interest in food and drink and so many different sources of information and education, from lavishly produced cookbooks to energetically presented TV cooking shows, people are beginning to see that with a little effort and discrimination, they can eat as well at home as any restaurant. And with a little imagination and a little drinks confidence on the side, they can have their friends thinking their place is the grooviest restaurant and bar in town!

Makes 1 drink

30ml / 1oz Rémy Martin Grand Cru Cognac

5ml / ¼oz Campari

5 chunks pineapple

10 mint leaves

2 teaspoons caster sugar

Piper-Heidsieck champagne, to top

coarse sugar rim, to garnish (see p 25)

pineapple leaf, to garnish

ice

Muddle shake and strain all ingredients, except champagne, into a chilled martini glass. Garnish with coarse sugar rim and pineapple leaf. See pages 30 and 33 for more on muddling, shaking and straining.

extractor

This is a little like the classic Greyhound, which uses vodka as a base instead of the tequila used in the Extractor. The tequila gives a more bitter and warming sensation, which, with the addition of Angostura bitters delivers a shorter and sharper bite.

Makes 1 drink

45ml / 1½oz Cuervo tequila

3-4 dashes Angostura bitters

60ml / 2oz Ocean Spray Ruby Red Grapefruit juice

slice of grapefruit, to garnish

ice

Shake all ingredients in ice-filled cocktail shaker. Pour into an ice-filled old-fashioned glass. Garnish with slice of grapefruit.

supper club

Every city in the world has a supper club, those late night venues serving finger food and cocktails late into the wee hours. Here's a very sexy drink you can make at home for your own late night gatherings.

Makes 1 drink

30ml / 1oz Grand Marnier

Piper-Heidsieck champagne, to top

5 raspberries

2 teaspoons caster sugar

ice

Muddle fruit in base of cocktail shaker with sugar. Add remaining ingredients, excluding champagne. Shake and strain ingredients into a chilled champagne flute. Top with champagne and garnish with raspberries. See page 30 for more on muddling, shaking and straining.

here is nothing like a good chandelier in every home

emerald eyes

Pineapple keeps almost everyone happy in a mixed drink. If you prefer a drier drink, consider using a more brut champagne or add a little Angostura bitters.

Makes 1 drink
30ml / 1oz Midori
15ml / ½oz South gin
30ml / 1oz pineapple juice
1 teaspoon caster sugar
Piper-Heidsieck champagne, to top
lime rind, to garnish
mint sprig, to garnish
ice

Shake and strain all ingredients, except champagne, into an ice-filled old-fashioned glass. Top with champagne. Garnish with lime rind. See page 30 for more on shaking and straining.

crystal loop

Makes 1 drink
30ml / 1oz Cuervo tequila
30ml / 1oz Ocean Spray Cranberry Classic juice
60ml / 2oz pineapple juice
4 raspberries
2 teaspoons caster sugar
Piper-Heidsieck champagne, to top
pineapple, thinly sliced, to garnish
ice

Muddle raspberries with sugar and cranberry juice in base of mixing glass. Add remaining ingredients except champagne. Shake and strain into ice-filled cocktail shaker. Pour into an ice-filled highball glass. Garnish with pineapple slice. See pages 30 and 33 for more on muddling, shaking and straining.

classic champagne cocktail

Makes 1 drink

2-3 dashes Angostura bitters

1 sugar cube

Piper-Heidsieck champagne, to top

Soak sugar cube in Angostura bitters and drop in a chilled champagne flute. Top with champagne.

songbird

Makes 1 drink

20ml / ¾oz Rémy Martin Grand Cru cognac

20ml / ¾oz Grand Marnier

15ml / ½oz grandberry glaze (see p 48)

3 raspberries

Piper Heidsieck champagne, to top

toffee mohawk, to garnish (see below)

ice

Muddle, shake and double strain all ingredients, except champagne, into an ice-filled old-fashioned glass, then top with champagne. Finish with a toffee mohawk garnish. See pages 30 and 33 for more on muddling, shaking and double straining.

toffee mohawk

1 cup sugar

1/3 cup water

1 teaspoon golden syrup

Bring ingredients to the boil and simmer for approximately 10 minutes. Test by dripping a drop of hot toffee into a glass of cold water: if it sets, it's time to lay toffee shapes. Lay grease-proof paper on a cool surface and drizzle toffee shapes.

solo step

Like the world famous all-time classic Mojito (see page 343) the tangy kiwifruit and mint in the Solo Step really cut through the sweetness, making a tantalising and refreshing pre-dinner drink. It's your first step towards a great evening.

Makes 1 drink

30ml / 1oz Havana Club Añejo Reserva rum

60ml / 2oz Ocean Spray White Cranberry juice

3-4 dashes Angostura bitters, to float

¼ pear, cored and chopped

½ kiwifruit, peeled and chopped

5 mint leaves

2 teaspoons sugar

soda water, to top

ice

Muddle kiwi, mint and sugar in base of mixing glass. Add remaining ingredients except soda water. Shake and pour unstrained into an ice-filled highball glass. See pages 30 and 33 for more on muddling, shaking and straining.

basilica

Makes 2 drinks

60ml / 2oz Midori

½ fresh lime, chopped

3 basil leaves

10 mint leaves

2 teaspoons sugar

ice

Muddle all ingredients in base of mixing glass. Shake and strain into chilled cocktail glasses. See pages 30 and 33 for more on muddling, shaking and straining.

jade

Often drinkers who are prefer sweet liqueurs find brut or dry champagne a little difficult to swallow. Using a sugar cube in the base will slowly release sweetness to the drink. The addition of sweet juicy fruits like pear or mango as an alternative will ensure a champagne-based cocktail almost anyone will enjoy. This is a luxuriously good example of the versatility of Midori with champagne.

Makes 1 drink

15ml / ½oz Midori

30ml / 1oz pear nectar

1 sugar cube

Piper-Heidsieck champagne, to top

Build ingredients in champagne flute.

party starter

Makes 1 drink

30ml / 1oz Cuervo tequila

30ml / 1oz apple, raspberry and vanilla glaze (see p 48)

Piper-Heidsieck champagne, to top

5 speared blueberries, to garnish

ice

Shake and strain tequila and glaze into a chilled martini glass. Top with champagne. Garnish with speared blueberries. See page 30 for more on shaking and straining.

stiletto

Makes 1 drink

30ml / 1oz Havana Club Añejo Blanco rum

30ml / 1oz sour apple liqueur (see p 159)

90ml / 3oz Ocean Spray White Cranberry juice

Piper-Heidsieck champagne, to top

large slice of apple, to garnish

ice

Shake and strain all ingredients, except champagne, into an ice-filled highball glass. Top with Piper Heidsieck champagne. Garnish with large slice of apple. See page 30 for more on shaking and straining.

dessert cocktails

Dessert cocktails often differ from other sweet cocktails in that they're usually cream or chocolate-based. However, I've also included a few fruitier creations such as the Batido-style cocktails using a sweetened meringue mix (see page 234). Dessert cocktails are a great way of perking everyone up after a sumptuous feast and they're often a delicious dessert in themselves, especially if everyone's stuffed!

cognac crème brulèe

Makes 1 drink

30ml / 1oz Grand Marnier

15ml / ¼oz Rémy Martin Grand Cru cognac

60ml / 2oz Ocean Spray White Cranberry Peach juice

1 chocolate cookie

2 teaspoons maple syrup, to sink

ice

Blend ingredients, except maple syrup, until smooth. Pour maple syrup into base of a chilled cocktail glass then pour drink on top.

chocolate granache

Makes 1 drink

15ml / ½oz Grand Marnier

60ml / 2oz Lipton Flavoured Black Tea Vanilla, steeped then chilled

45ml / 1½oz white chocolate and raspberry liqueur (see p 155)

½ pear, cored chopped

2 teaspoons caster sugar

chocolate curls, to garnish (see p 240)

ice

Blend ingredients until smooth then pour into cocktail glass. Garnish with chocolate curls, which you can make by grating a block of good 80% cocoa cooking chocolate. Alternatively you can simply use a dusting of powdered drinking chocolate.

pecan praline

Makes 1 drink

30ml / 1oz Havana Club Añejo Reserva rum

30ml / 1oz pecan pear crème liqueur (see p 162)

60ml / 2oz Ocean Spray White Cranberry juice

30ml / 1oz espresso coffee

30ml / 1oz half 'n' half (see p 41)

2 pecan nuts, ground, to garnish

chocolate topping, to garnish

ice

Blend all ingredients, except pecan nuts, until smooth. Pour into a chilled cocktail glass. Garnish with chocolate topping and ground pecan rim. For more on rimming glasses see page 25.

cinnamon flip

This is an after dinner or dessert-style cocktail. Using Lipton Cinnamon and Apple Herbal Infusion offers a bold range of flavours to mix with. This is a light and delicate drink that has a very special flavour of apple and spice.

Makes 1 drink

45ml / 1½oz Havana Club Añejo Reserva rum

15ml / ½oz Grand Marnier

30ml / 1oz Lipton Cinnamon and Apple Herbal Infusion, steeped and chilled

30ml / 1oz sweet 'n' sour mix (see p 40)

20ml / ¾oz maple syrup

1 egg white

ground cinnamon, to garnish

apple slice, to garnish

ice

Shake and strain all ingredients into a chilled martini glass. Garnish with ground cinnamon and apple slice.

caramel coffee trifle

Makes 1 drink

45ml / 1¼oz Havana Club Añejo Blanco rum

15ml / ½oz Frangelico

30ml / 1oz caramel topping

30ml / 1oz espresso coffee, chilled

1 large scoop vanilla ice cream

coconut, desiccated, to garnish

cocoa dusting, to garnish

ice

Blend ingredients until smooth then pour into a chilled cocktail glass. Garnish with long desiccated coconut and a dusting of cocoa.

berry blitz torte

Granita-style dessert cocktails are a great way to cleanse the palate, particularly after rich meals. The Berry Blitz Torte is slightly tart. Tartness can be increased by adding more lime or decreasing sugar.

Makes 1 drink

30ml / 1oz Remy Martin Grand Cru cognac

15ml / ½oz Midori

15ml / ½oz framboise

60ml / 2oz Ocean Spray Cranberry Classic juice

30ml / 1oz lime juice

3 raspberries

2 strawberries, pruned and chopped

2 teaspoons caster sugar

strawberry, to garnish

ice

Blend ingredients until smooth then pour into a chilled cocktail glass. Garnish with strawberry.

berry blitz torte, rum raisin poco

rum raisin poco

Sweeten up after dinner with a little poco-ing around. Using simple ingredients like chocolate topping and orange make this drink really easy to prepare. Take a little time to whip up the rum raisin glaze (see page 46) beforehand to make it really special. You'll be amazed at how yummy this drink tastes... and besides, we all prefer sweetening up to cleaning up!

Makes 1 drink
30ml / 1oz Havana Club Añejo Blanco rum
30ml / 1oz rum raisin glaze (see p 46)
60ml / 2oz freshly juiced orange juice
30ml / 1oz chocolate topping
orange rind, to garnish
ice

Shake all ingredients in ice-filled cocktail shaker. Pour into an ice-filled highball glass. Garnish with orange rind.

pear, passionfruit flyte

Makes 1 drink
30ml / 1oz Grand Marnier
30ml / 1oz South gin
30ml / 1oz Lipton Lychee, Lime and Passionfruit Herbal Infusion, steeped and chilled
30ml / 1oz sweet 'n' sour mix (see p 40)
30ml / 1oz passionfruit pulp
½ pear, cored and chopped
2 teaspoons sugar
ice

Pour passionfruit pulp into base of a chilled cocktail glass. Blend remaining ingredients until smooth and pour over passionfruit pulp.

baklava crème

Makes 1 drink

30ml / 1oz 42 Below vodka (Optional 42 Below Manuka Honey vodka)

30ml / 1oz pecan pear crème liqueur (see p 162)

60ml / 2oz mango nectar

30ml / 1oz half 'n' half (see p 41)

2 teaspoons caster sugar

honey and chopped walnut rim, to garnish (see p 25)

ice

Blend ingredients until smooth then pour into a chilled cocktail glass. Garnish with honey and chopped walnut rim (see page 25).

strawberry sponge

Makes 1 drink

15ml / ½oz Grand Marnier

30ml / 1oz framboise

15ml / ½oz Frangelico

30ml / 1oz half 'n' half (see p 41)

60ml / 2oz Ocean Spray White Cranberry Strawberry juice

1 strawberry slice, to garnish

ice

Shake all ingredients in ice-filled cocktail shaker. Strain into a chilled martini glass. Garnish with strawberry slice.

batido dessert cocktails

This is one of the most impressive little cocktails you can make - and one of the simplest. It looks very much like a dessert, based on the wonderful South American dessert of the same name which I was introduced to by my beautiful wife Esmeralda, whose family hails from Colombia.

The batido is a traditional treat which is made in the same way as the recipe below. The only exception is that traditional batido includes cinnamon. Historically, the cinnamon version is enjoyed without any additional ingredients after dinner on Fridays to celebrate the coming of the weekend.

However, using the basic batido mix recipe and method below as a base, you'll only be limited by your imagination in making simple but delicious dessert cocktails that pack a very relaxing punch.

batido - recipe

Makes 200ml / 7oz, or approximately 2 drinks
1 egg white
1 egg yolk
1½ tablespoons caster sugar

batido - method

The most important thing to remember when making batido mix is to keep the bowl and beater completely dry - make sure no water or other liquids enter the bowl or splash the beater as moisture prohibits its wonderful gelatinous consistency from forming.

In a dry bowl beat egg whites and caster sugar for 2-3 minutes until fluffy. The mixture should have the consistency of uncooked meringue, or stiff fluffy white peaks - a good indication that the mix is ready is if you can turn the bowl quickly upside-down with the mix in it and mix won't stays firmly in place. Add yolks and slowly beat again for a further 30 seconds.

Layer batido mixture over cocktail. As ice or other liquid will deplete its fluffy texture, make drinks in two parts. Shake and strain or blend ingredients and alcohol together for the base - then layer batido mix on top forming a decadent and delicious crown for the cocktail.

passionfruit, mango batido

Makes 2 drinks

60ml / 2oz Havana Club Añejo Blanco rum

60ml / 2oz mango nectar

60ml / 2oz passionfruit pulp

2 teaspoons caster sugar

3 tablespoons batido mix (see p 234), to top each glass

passionfruit pulp, to garnish

ice

Shake and strain ingredients, except batido mix, into chilled cocktail glasses. Float batido mix on top of cocktail in glasses by gently spooning it on. Garnish with passionfruit pulp.

rum raisin batido

Makes 2 drinks

60ml / 2oz Grand Marnier

60ml / 2oz Ocean Spray Cranberry Classic juice

60ml / 2oz rum raisin glaze (see p 46)

3 tablespoons batido mix (see p 234), to top each glass

cinnamon, ground, to garnish

ice

Shake and strain ingredients except batido mix into chilled cocktail glasses. Float batido mix on top of cocktail in glasses by gently spooning it on. Garnish with a dusting of cinnamon.

um raisin batido, white berry chocolate batido

whip one

white berry chocolate batido

Making the final product look good is half the objective of preparing a quality cocktail. By using the blade of a sharp knife and scraping the chocolate from the flat side of the block, chocolate curls are formed.

Makes 2 drinks
60ml / 2oz 42 Below vodka
30ml / 1oz Ocean Spray White Cranberry juice
3 tablespoons batido mix (see p 234), to top each glass
white chocolate curls, to garnish (see below)
ice

Shake and strain ingredients except batido mix into chilled cocktail glasses. Float batido mix on top of cocktail in glasses by gently spooning it on. Garnish with chocolate curls.

Making chocolate curls is easy. Lay a bar of chocolate face down on a clean cutting board. Press the blade of a large carving knife firmly onto the flat, or back of, a bar of chocolate. While holding the chocolate bar still, pull the blade towards yourself scraping the chocolate with the knife. The more firm the pressure of the knife, the thicker the curls.

zesty lime and honey batido

Makes 2 drinks

60ml / 2oz 42 Below Manuka Honey vodka

60ml / 2oz Ocean Spray White Cranberry juice

60ml / 2oz liquid honey

¼ lime zest, grated

3 tablespoons batido mix (see p 234), to top each glass

sugar rim, to garnish

ice

Shake and strain ingredients except batido mix into chilled cocktail glasses. Float batido mix on top of cocktail in glasses by gently spooning it on. Garnish with sugar rim (see page 25).

orange, strawberry slice batido

Makes 2 drinks

45ml / 1½oz Cuervo tequila

15ml / ½oz Midori

60ml / 2oz freshly juiced orange juice

2 strawberries, sliced finely

2 teaspoons caster sugar

3 tablespoons batido mix (see p 234), to top each glass

ice

Muddle strawberries with orange juice and sugar then add remaining ingredients except batido mix. Shake and strain ingredients into chilled cocktail glasses. Layer batido mix over cocktail in glass.

banana, coconut batido

Makes 2 drinks

90ml / 3oz Ocean Spray White Cranberry juice

15ml / ½oz orange ginger glaze (see p 47)

1 banana, peeled

1 teaspoon coconut essence

3 tablespoons batido mix (see p 234), to top each glass

ice

Muddle fruit in base of cocktail shaker with glaze, then add remaining ingredients. Shake and double strain into chilled cocktail glasses. Layer batido mix over cocktail in glass. For more on muddling, shaking and double straining see pages 30 and 33.

coffees and milkshakes

From the steaming coffee houses of Milan to the Turkish coffee stalls at bus stations in Istanbul - I do love a cuppa joe. But for the flair bartender in me, it's not as much about whether the coffee's the finest in the world, or whether the equipment has all the bells and whistles… it's cafeteria theatre that blows me away.

To watch as a barista (or coffee maker) bashes out six to eight hundred coffees a day. The fluid motion as they drive a four cup machine to peak performance. As the wilting customer is suddenly perked up with an injection of energy. Or how coffee can take over a bar as a night spot - I've seen coffee shops packed with a crowd guzzling coffee at 1am.

Although most places in the world where good coffee is found prefer their coffee short, black and strong, coffee's popularity in places like Australia and America has been helped along by milky coffees like the caffé latté or flat white. You can't start a Roman morning without a cappuccino, or a Parisian one without a boule of café au lait. Although coffee was very popular in England and America in the 1700s, it was overtaken by tea after the Ceylonese coffee blight of the mid 1800s. However, while it's still sometimes tricky to get a decent coffee in New York or London, coffee and café culture have suddenly become all the rage, mainly due to the popularity of milky coffee. Today, over eighty percent of coffee drunk in the West is made with milk.

Which brings me to milkshakes. Before cafés became popular, the drugstore, milk bar or dairy (in NZ) was the place to hang out. I love those funky old milkshake mixers, the tall chrome shake cup, the bendy oversized straws… although the milk bar may be dying out in favour of the café, the milkshake is an institution.

secrets to the perfect cup

There is nothing quite like the feeling of being able to make better coffee in your home than the café down the road. Here are a few helpful suggestions to turn your home into your own special café:

what to look for when buying a coffee machine?

Try to invest in a home espresso machine. A good machine I like to use is the Sunbeam Café Series Coffee machine. With so much interest in coffee and coffee making, there's been an explosion of readily available machines launched on the market and available in most good department and electrical stores. They can range in price from around $150 all the way up to deluxe models that can cost up to $2,500! However, you can still get reasonable results from a less expensive machine, as long as you look for the following things:

- At least 15 bar pump pressure - to ensure that steam is produced at the right pressure and can froth milk effectively
- A good milk frothing arm
- A good size water tank - at least 1.5L / 3 pints will ensure you don't run out of steam or water while making coffees

To get the best from your coffee machine, you should always try to use only freshly-ground coffee. So consider investing in a coffee grinder, especially one with the following features:

- Easily disassembled for easier cleaning - including easy access to the ground drawer (you don't want to make a mess while grinding coffee!)
- A range of grinding options, from superfine to coarse - you don't need lots of grinding options, but make sure that the fine grind is sufficiently fine

The grind of coffee is critical. Use a fine to medium grind for domestic espresso machines. This provides a good compression of the coffee in the group head and thus, produces a quality crèma on top of the coffee.

care for your coffee

Many amateur baristas make the mistake of either not storing coffee in an airtight container in a cool, dark place like the cupboard - leaving it out unsealed will make it stale; leaving it in the freezer doesn't keep it fresher but in fact freezes its natural oils (and taste).

Keep your espresso machine clean and thoroughly rinsed. Run water through the brewing head and flush the steaming nozzle in fresh water after each use. Always follow the manufacturer's instructions for cleaning and care, including regular decalcification to ensure that all the plumbing works cleanly and clearly.

buying coffee

Always use the freshest beans or ground coffee available and store in an airtight container in a cool, dry, dark place. With so many varieties and roasts it's hard to suggest which one is best. Part of coffee culture is to find your own preferred bean at a coffee roaster or café. Talk to the roaster and be passionate about your beans. You'll make good friends with coffee roasters as they're very excitable with all that caffeine bursting through their veins.

Only grind beans as you need them and don't leave them in the grinder - this will make them stale.

making good coffee

A single shot of espresso should result in only 30-45ml / 1 - 1¼oz of coffee.

A common mistake is running too much water through the ground coffee, resulting in a thin and bitter-tasting espresso. Drawing 30ml / 1oz will extract around as much flavour and essence from the coffee as 60ml / 2oz will. The difference is simple: more water and greater volume.

Ensure your coffee grinds are 'tamped' evenly. 'Tamping' refers to the amount of pressure with which coffee grinds are packed into the filter. Packing them in firmly will also give you a better tasting coffee and the water will be extracting more from the coffee under pressure.

steaming milk

Always use cold milk and a clean stainless steel jug when steaming. Skim milk or milk that has less full cream in it will froth easier as the milk fats can render low aeration of milk. You might consider frothing milk with equal half measures of full cream and skim milk, or the new varieties of 'cappuccino' milk, specifically made for cappuccino frothing.

Don't boil the milk when steaming. The best way to avoid this is by first ensuring that the frother is not blocked. Run the frother for a 3-5 seconds to remove obstructions. Keep the nozzle just under the surface of the milk to start, then plunge it to the bottom of the jug as the pressure builds. Keep the jug moving gently up and down, until the jug becomes slightly too hot to touch. Watch out for the milk boiling; you can check this by sniffing the jug from time to time until you become experienced enough to know the right temperature. If it's steaming, it's probably too late! But don't worry, practice does make perfect. Alternatively, you might consider investing in a special cooking or milk-frothing thermometer used by professional baristas and found in any good coffee supply shop. It has special markings to tell you easily when your milk is approaching the danger zone!

A good method to condense the steamed milk after steaming is to tap the bottom of the steamer jug. By either doing this with your hand or by tapping the base of the jug on a folded tea towel on the kitchen bench, results is a more dense frothed milk. Just like in a good café. You may also wish to use skimmed milk as this makes for a much frothier head, but the milk underneath may be a little thin compared to whole milk.

Little things count - warming your cups, using filtered water
and serving the coffee immediately after brewing do make a difference.

draw

Getting the most out of the coffee and extracting the maximum flavour is the most important art to being a good barista. Press the ground coffee in the group handle - or coffee filter cup - very hard before fitting in the group and drawing the water. Also, it's good to know the amount of coffee to have in the group handle to make the correct level when pressed so it meets the filter in the coffee head. This means a good packed group handle of ground coffee will extract the most goodness when drawn. And always ensure you use only fresh filtered water!

café coffee

Every café will tell you that their coffee is made better, tastes better and looks better than everyone else's. And while this might be true in some cases, here's a sure way of making coffees at home - with a little help from the tips above - to ensure that you can make café-standard coffee at home and blow the cappuccino froth off a few hot surprises for your friends when they pop over for a coffee.

short black	30 - 45ml or 1 - 1½oz espresso served in a short cup or glass
long black	60 - 75ml or 2 - 2½oz espresso served in a normal coffee cup
flat white	(milky coffee) - 60ml / 2oz espresso topped with steamed milk, served in a normal coffee cup
café latté (Café au lait)	- 30ml / 1oz espresso topped with steamed milk, served in a 150ml / 5oz café glass
bowl latté	90ml / 3oz espresso topped with a generous 200ml / 7oz steamed milk, served in a large bowl
cappuccino	30ml / 1oz espresso topped with extra frothy steamed milk. If you pour in steamed milk to fill the cup and let it set for a few moments, it can then be topped further raising the level of the froth to form the iconic cappuccino look. Dust with cocoa (Australian) or cinnamon (American). Italians prefer it without any dusting or further adornment
macchiato	30ml / 1oz of espresso stained (macchiato means stained in Italian), with a teaspoon of steamed milk
vienna	60ml / 2oz espresso with a large spoon of whipped cream added
afogatto	60ml / 2oz espresso poured over 1 or 2 scoops of vanilla ice cream

Sweeten coffee to taste with sugar. I prefer brown sugar as it has a slight caramel flavour when stirred into the right hot coffee. You may also use raw sugar or coffee crystals. For more on sugar see Sugar Daddy on page 18 in the Methods and Hip Things chapter.

honeybee café mocha

Made in a similar way to a cappuccino but with the addition of drinking chocolate. Simply stir the chocolate into the espresso prior to adding the steamed milk and froth.

Makes 1 drink

30 - 60ml / 1 - 2oz espresso

30ml / 1oz banana coconut glaze (see p 47)

2 teaspoons of drinking chocolate

steamed milk, to top

chocolate curls, to garnish (see p 240)

cocoa powder dusting, to garnish

Add espresso to a 190 - 240ml / approx. 6½oz cup or highball glass. Stir drinking chocolate and glaze into espresso prior to adding the steamed milk and froth. Garnish with chocolate curls and dust with cocoa powder. For more on dusting see page 36.

rum raisin macchiato

Traditionally served as a standard espresso with a dash of milk and a small dollop of froth into the middle of the 'crema', macchiato is Italian for 'to stain or mark'. Try it with a small amount of glaze (see p 44) and try a dolce macchiato.

Makes 1 drink

30 - 60ml / 1 - 2oz espresso

steamed milk froth to stain

20ml / ¾oz rum raisin glaze (see p 46)

Pour espresso into 90ml / 3oz espresso glass or demitasse cup. Then add glaze followed by dash of steamed milk.

cognac schnapps mocha coffee

Make 1 drink

30ml / 1oz espresso, freshly drawn

30ml / 1oz Rémy Martin Grand Cru cognac

1 teaspoon cocoa powder

2 teaspoon sugar

1 cup milk, frothed

1 tablespoon cream, freshly whipped

cocoa powder, to garnish

Mix cocoa powder, cognac, sugar and coffee to create a paste in bottom of a tall highball glass. Pour frothed milk and add a dollop of whipped cream. Garnish with chocolate dusting. See page 36 for more on dusting.

Liqueur coffees are delicious and make for great nightcaps. Be sure to let your friends know what they are drinking and the quantity of alcohol in the drink.

tequila vanilla coffee

Using whipped full cream in liqueur coffees gives them a very rich flavour. You can tone a liqueur coffee down by lowering the quantity of alcohol and sugar.

Makes 2 drinks

45ml / 1½oz Cuervo tequila

15ml / ½oz Galliano Vanilla

200ml / 6½oz espresso, freshly drawn

2 tablespoons cream, freshly whipped

200ml / 6½oz milk, frothed (see p 250)

2 teaspoons sugar

split vanilla bean, to garnish

cocoa powder, to garnish (see p 36)

Build ingredients in an old-fashioned glass. Garnish with a dusting of cocoa and split vanilla bean.

zion

Makes 1 drink

20ml / ¾oz sweetened condensed milk

20ml / ¾oz espresso, freshly drawn

20ml / ¾oz 42 Below Manuka Honey vodka

Layer ingredients in order listed, in small cocktail glass.

grand espresso

Makes 1 drink

15ml / ½oz Grand Marnier

30ml / 1oz espresso, freshly drawn

2 teaspoon sugar

orange zest

Place orange zest and sugar in a short glass with Grand Marnier. Bruise or twist orange zest a little with the back of a spoon while dissolving sugar. Pour espresso on top and serve.

When using orange zest, twist or bruise it so the oils are expelled to the drink adding citrus aromas.

tequila bon bon

Makes 4 drinks

20ml / ¾oz sweetened condensed milk

20ml / ¾oz espresso, freshly drawn

20ml / ¾oz Cuervo tequila

Layer ingredients in order listed, in small cocktail glass.

melon bon bon

Makes 4 drinks

20ml / ¾oz sweetened condensed milk

20ml / ¾oz Midori

20ml / ¾oz espresso, freshly drawn

Layer ingredients in order listed, in small cocktail glass.

honeycomb express

Makes 1 drink

45ml / 1½oz Midori

15ml / ½oz Grand Marnier

30ml / 1oz maple syrup

60ml / 2oz espresso, freshly drawn

cocoa powder, to garnish

crushed chocolate honeycomb, to garnish

ice

Shake and strain ingredients from cocktail shaker into a chilled martini glass. Garnish with a dusting of cocoa and crushed chocolate honeycomb.

grand lacroix

This is a fantastically decadent late night coffee drink. Lacroix is the crème de la crème of liqueur coffees and what better way to enjoy Grand Marnier than in a late night nightcap?

Makes 1 drink

45ml / 1¼oz Grand Marnier

30ml / 1oz espresso coffee

2 teaspoons cream, whipped

sugar to taste

1 orange rind, zested, to garnish

Pour freshly drawn espresso and Cointreau into a liqueur glass. Dollop whipped cream over ingredients and garnish with fine orange rind. See page 26 for more on citrus rind.

golden marshmallow

Makes 1 drink

15ml / ½oz Galliano Vanilla

45ml / 1½oz espresso, freshly drawn

1 teaspoon sugar

2 marshmallows

Preheat your glasses with hot water for 1 minute before discarding the water and drying. Warm glasses keep drinks hot for longer. Dissolve sugar with Galliano in a small wine glass. Add marshmallows and pour hot espresso over ingredients. Allow marshmallows to soften for a short time before drinking.

easy rider

Makes 1 drink

30ml / 1oz Rémy Martin Grand Cru cognac

30ml / 1oz Frangelico

30ml / 1oz full cream

30ml / 1oz espresso

2 teaspoons caster sugar

1 teaspoon orange grated rind

chocolate topping, to garnish

ice

Blend all ingredients until smooth and pour into a chilled cocktail glass. Garnish with chocolate topping. When blending a drink ensure your glassware is chilled before pouring the blended drink. This can easily be done by first filling your glass with ice and discarding prior to pouring.

café snap

Makes 1 drink

60ml / 2oz espresso

20ml / ¾oz golden syrup

1 teaspoon whipped cream

Pour espresso into 90ml / 3oz espresso glass or demitasse cup. Then add golden syrup and layer on top whipped cream.

raspberry coffee spider

Makes 1 drink

30ml / 1oz raspberry cordial

60ml / 2oz espresso, freshly drawn

2 scoops hazelnut gelato

1 teaspoon sugar

lemonade, to top

ice

Build ingredients in order listed in a sundae glass.

choc coffee spider

Makes 1 drink

30ml / 1oz chocolate topping

60ml / 2oz espresso, freshly drawn

2 scoops vanilla gelato

1 teaspoon sugar

cola, to top

ice

Build ingredients in order listed in a sundae glass.

milkshakes

The traditional milkshake's two main ingredients are thick syrup added to ice-cold milk and shaking the concoction up in a shaker, much like a cocktail. With the advent of the milk bar in the 1950s, came the spindle, or flash-mixer. This allowed busy milk bars to serve milkshakes in a flash without the fuss or delay of hand-shaking.

I think old fashioned chromed flash-mixers are very cool pieces of equipment which look fantastic on a kitchen bench. Plus, they do encourage a fun and delicious way to drink more milk.

With these recipes, I've tried to incorporate as many fresh ingredients as I could, including kiwi fruit, banana and mint. Most of the sweeteners listed can be changed according to preference. For example, honey can be substituted for sugar, maple syrup swapped for golden syrup, and so on. This way it's easier to control the sugars in some of the drinks, but I've also left the option to go berserk with toppings. It's up to you.

Making shakes in a flash mixer requires a milk bar cup, which is a metal cup that looks a lot like a cocktail shaker, except that it's wider and more robust. These are the traditional metal cups in which shakes are served in milk bars and cafés. Although you may wish to drink with two straws in the milk bar cup, I prefer evenly pouring the shake into a couple of highballs. Don't worry about fancy garnishes as milkshakes are all about the flavour - and the slurp! It's actually considered good manners to give the cup one last might slurp to share that satisfying sound with everyone. Really!

If you don't have a flash milk bar appliance, you can mix these just as easily in a blender. However, make sure you use only chilled ingredients and not ice to prevent diluting the shake and making it watery. Another alternative is to shake them up in cocktail shaker without ice. If this is your preferred method, don't strain the drink as it would take a long time with all the thick, pulpy ingredients... not to mention the fun of drinking it!

orange, mint and honey shake

Makes 2 drinks
300ml / 10oz milk, chilled
30ml / 1oz liquid honey
1 cup mint leaves, juiced
2 oranges juiced
sprig of mint, to garnish

Juice mint, followed by oranges, to flush mint flavours through juicer. Add ingredients to milk bar cup and flash mix for 30 seconds. Pour into highball glasses. Garnish with mint sprig.

kiwi, banana and maple shake

Tangy yet mellow.

Makes 2 drinks
300ml / 10oz milk, chilled
30ml / 1oz maple syrup
2 bananas, juiced
4 kiwi fruit, juiced
kiwi fruit wheel, to garnish

Juice bananas, followed by kiwis to flush banana flavours through juicer. Add ingredients to milk bar cup and flash mix for 30 seconds. Pour into highball glasses. Garnish with kiwi fruit wheel.

shimmy shake

Makes 2 drinks
300ml / 10oz milk, chilled
30ml / 1oz maple syrup
1 cup raspberries, juiced
2 pears, juiced

Juice raspberries, followed by pears, to flush raspberry flavours through juicer. Add ingredients to milk bar cup and flash mix for 30 seconds. Pour into highball glasses.

mango, banana and cinnamon shake

Warming with cinnamon, but cool with milk and sweet with mango. This is a sort of a 'Sunday evening on the couch' shake.

Makes 2 drinks

300ml / 10oz milk, chilled

2 bananas juiced or blended

2 mangoes, juiced or 100ml / 3½oz mango nectar

½ teaspoon cinnamon, ground

ground cinnamon, to garnish

cinnamon quill, to garnish

Juice bananas, followed by mangoes to flush banana juices through juicer. Add ingredients to milk bar cup and flash mix for 30 seconds. Pour into highball glasses. Garnish with dusting of ground cinnamon and cinnamon stick.

honey, vanilla and rockmelon shake

Makes 2 drinks

300ml / 10oz milk, chilled

30ml / 1oz liquid honey

¼ rockmelon, juiced

1 vanilla bean, split and scrapped

Juice rockmelon. Add ingredients to milk bar cup and flash mix for 30 seconds. Pour into highball glasses.

caramel, peach and ginger shake

Sweet succulent and tangy with a warm bite of ginger.

Makes 2 drinks
300ml / 10oz milk, chilled
30ml / 1oz caramel topping
2 peaches, juiced
2cm knob ginger, juiced

Juice ginger, followed by peaches to flush through the flavours of the ginger through the juicer. Add ingredients to milk bar cup and flash mix for 30 seconds. Pour into highball glasses.

double chocoholic shake

Anyone who loves chocolate 'double-loves' a chocolate milkshake! It's a refreshingly rich get-up-and-go-go for those who might not like coffee.

Makes 2 drinks
300ml / 10oz milk, chilled
2 tablespoons cocoa powder
30ml / 1oz chocolate topping
2 teaspoons maple syrup
cocoa dusting and your favourite chocolate bar, to garnish

Add ingredients to milk bar cup and flash mix for 30-60 seconds. Pour into highball glasses. Garnish with chocolate dusting and your favourite chocolate bar.

take the plunge

With our lives so much busier we all know the difficulty of choosing the right setting to catch up with a friend and just talk. Lunch is usually a rushed bite between meetings, dinner always a little too late, and shouting over the music or trying to find a seat in a crowded club can be impossible.

A nice alternative to the above might be High Tea. And we're not talking about a teabag on a barstool - we're talking the WHOLE shebang. The High Tea Experience is popular in many fashionable bars, and was made famous at the Ritz in London. High Tea involves not just tea (obviously) but an appetising selection of little delicacies such as sandwiches, pastries and other snacks.

Before you start going on about old ladies with cats and the fact that you only use your tea cosy as head adornment when you're skiing, it's not as stuffy as it sounds!

As I mentioned above - before the cats and tea cosies - it's becoming fashionable in many trendy clubs and bars. And what could be more enjoyable or memorable for you and your friends than entertaining in a unique way? If you're looking for High Tea with a splash of difference and something not too stiff upper lip, try a Tea Tisane, Café Piña Colada or a Café Cosmo - Green Tea with Raspberries, lime and hot cranberry juice.

What is the official time for tea, you ask? Well, although dinner's replaced the original time for High Tea - which was six o'clock in the evening - it's traditionally been considered four o'clock since Anna, Duchess of Bedford, found herself feeling faint in the afternoon. Sipping a little tea to tide her over until dinner time, she ordered the servants to bring some light refreshments and nibbles to snack on while she drank her tea. Once her aristocratic chums realised they too could enjoy a little munch in the dead hours before dinner, they started coming round and enjoying the little ritual the Duchess had invented.

If you're neither punctual nor a stickler, High Tea may be taken at any time in the afternoon, and may be used as a replacement for supper. This is because a bit more food is served at High Tea than at Afternoon Tea.

High Tea Time is more adaptable to allow for the best time for your guests to be free, and so you'll have extra time for cricket, or bridge, or whatever takes your fancy.

So, whether it's Mozart or Metallica that helps you to unwind, escort your guests into the atmosphere you wish to create. It pays to go a little further and add a suave touch by adding a cocktail to the end of your High Tea experience. It's the modern day lubricant to entertaining chit chat.

Try a Banjo Martini (page 174) - a sultry mix of vodka, pomegranate and cranberry peach juice; or a Apple Groove Tequini (page 185) - smooth as a groove with tequila, bitters and apple sweetened and mixed with white cranberry juice.

For a hip and groovy High Tea experience be sure to have modern tea accessories, comfy chairs and a centrally located table for tea-making and all the lovely food and cocktails. Remember to avoid crocheted doilies under your plates! And, you and your friends will be sure to feel fabalicious.

steep

Getting the best of tea makes the world of difference when it comes to the final cup. In a modern world of instant everything, gradual steeping is often overlooked as the old-fashioned practice of grandmas and grandads. Yet the recent popularity of chic tea boutiques reveal that more and more people are discovering the benefits of tea, and noticing the difference between a dashed two minute dangle and a proper five minute steep. It's a world of difference between tannin-flavoured hot water and a great cup of tea.

In this chapter, you may find some descriptions and terms that are unfamiliar. Here are some of the terms and phrases used:

Fruit Flavoured Green Tea - Based on traditional green teas, these can be found in bags, flavoured with fruits like mango or watermelon. Unlike other teas, Fruit Flavoured Green Tea suits sweet fruit flavours as it's not as bitter, making the resulting combination very refreshing.

Herbal Infusions - Now available in bags but also available loose-leaf, these use herbs rather than tea, and are thus caffeine-free. Many not only taste good and make a nice change from tea, but they have reputed health benefits. Everyone knows a nice cup of chamomile tea is a great sleep aid;

but did you know peppermint tea is excellent for digestion and upset tummies? Herbal Infusions are usually drunk without milk, to best enjoy the clarity and intensity of the flavours.

Tea Tisane - A tisane is a brew of fresh or dried fruits in hot water. Adding tea to this creates a tea-like cocktail I call a Tea Tisane (or is that a cocktail-style tea?). This innovative combination allows you to be more creative with flavours and styling, while still ending up with a refreshing and intriguing hot brew. For iced tea, simply chill the Tea Tisane and enjoy over ice.

Black Flavoured Tea - Available in bags in flavours like chai, cookies and cream or hazelnut, these are black teas with quality flavouring. To be enjoyed with or without milk and can be enjoyed as a latté experience with the pump and pour - plunger frothing technique (see p 291)

Dry Tea Mix - Created with loose-leaf tea and other ingredients. A good example is Mumbai Jumbo Chai (see p 292)

plunger or tea pot brew - method

Add two teaspoons of tea per cup to plunger or tea pot - so if making two cups, use four teaspoons. Pour one cup of boiling water per cup.

plungers - plunge three to four times to circulate tea then leave for three to five minutes.
tea pots - turn pot 3 times clockwise (that's Gran's suggestion) and leave for 3-5 minutes.
Steeping for 3-5 minutes will intensify the flavours of the brew. Some prefer a little longer, depending on preferred strength. Add sweetener (where applicable) to taste.

Although a plunger isn't necessary for a tea bag, if it's your choice of vessel and you only have tea bags, substitute one tea bag to every two teaspoons of loose leaf tea.

With the exception of chai tea, herbal and fruit teas don't require milk as their flavour is more refined when enjoyed with just hot water and perhaps a little sugar or honey.

tea tisanes

café piña colada

The all-time classic cocktail Piña Colada can be remixed to suit a lazy Sunday brunch. This is a groovy alternative drink guaranteed to satisfy.

Makes 4 drinks

2 bags Lipton Green Tea with Jasmine

5 chunks pineapple, chopped finely

1 tablespoon coconut, desiccated

1 teaspoon, maple syrup or honey per cup

480ml / 16oz boiling water

Add ingredients to plunger or tea pot and steep for 3-5 minutes before pouring into tea cups. Sweeten with maple syrup or honey.

hot orchard tea tisane

Making creative tea is adventurous and adds a culinary spark to a glass. It's by far more exciting than pouring up a simple cup of tea. Adding new ingredients to your tea gives a personal touch to your brew.

Makes 4 drinks

2 bags Lipton Lemon Herbal Infusion

3 kaffir lime leaves

1 plum, cut into wheels

1 lime, cut into wheels

1 teaspoon honey per cup

480ml / 16oz boiling hot water

Add ingredients to a plunger or tea pot and steep for 3-5 minutes before pouring into tea cups. Sweeten with maple syrup or honey.

café cosmo

The Cosmopolitan - or Cosmo, as it's affectionately known - is an ever-popular hit in cocktail bars around the world. It's always nice to give classics a bit of a shake up, even if they become the opposite: a non-alcoholic hot drink that can be enjoyed in the morning!

Makes 4 drinks

2 bags Lipton Lemon Herbal Infusion

200ml / 6½oz Ocean Spray Cranberry Classic juice, hot

5 raspberries

1 lime, juiced

1 lime cut into wheels

1 teaspoon honey per cup

280ml / 9½oz boiling water

Add ingredients to plunger or teapot and steep for 3-5 minutes before pouring into tea cups. Sweeten with maple syrup or honey.

tropical star buster

Tropical flavours of pineapple mixed with exotic star anise makes for an exciting cup of mix-and-match tea.

Makes 4 drinks

2 bags Lipton Green Tea with Jasmine

1 tablespoon dried pineapple

1 tablespoon dried pawpaw

1 tablespoon star anise, dried and crushed

2 lemons, grated zest

480ml / 16oz boiling water

Add ingredients to plunger or tea pot and steep for 3-5 minutes before pouring into tea cups. Sweeten with maple syrup or honey.

thai kick

Fruity tea tisanes are the quintessentially refreshing hot drink. They not only look like they'll quench a desert thirst, with tea they'll give you a brilliant lift and spark too.

Makes 4 drinks

2 bags Lipton Green Tea with Mango

½ lemongrass stem, split

3 fresh kaffir lime leaves

1 teaspoon honey per cup

480ml / 16oz boiling water

Add ingredients to plunger or tea pot and steep for 3-5 minutes before pouring into tea cups. Sweeten with maple syrup or honey.

royal geisha

Makes 4 drinks

2 bags Lipton Green Tea with Mango

2 tablespoons sultanas

1 lemongrass stem, split

5 star anise

1 teaspoon honey per cup

480ml / 16oz boiling water

Add ingredients to plunger or tea pot and steep for 3-5 minutes before pouring into tea cups. Sweeten with honey.

WAITERS
CROSSING

CONTINENTAL
CAKES
TO TAKE AWAY

vanilla, apricot and honey tea tisane

Makes 4 drinks

2 bags Lipton Green Tea with Honey

4 dried apricots, chopped

1 vanilla bean, split and scraped then chopped finely

1 teaspoon honey per cup, optional

480ml / 16oz boiling water

Add ingredients to a plunger or tea pot and steep for 2-3 minutes before pouring into tea cups. Sweeten with honey to taste.

apricot cha cha

Apricots are a summer stone fruit but are available dried in packets from the supermarket all year round. Mixing-and-matching your own apricot tea tisane will keep you dancing the cha cha all day long.

Makes 4 drinks

2 bags Lipton Green Tea with Jasmine

4 dried apricots, chopped finely

1 teaspoon, maple syrup or honey per cup

½ lime, grated zest

½ orange, grated zest

480ml / 16oz boiling hot water

Add ingredients to a plunger or tea pot and steep for 2-3 minutes before pouring into tea cups. Sweeten with maple syrup or honey.

hindi chai - english tea

Chai is Hindi for tea. A spicy, sweet, usually milky concoction using black tea as a base for more flavours, it's the national drink of India, served in delicate steaming glasses and cups, drunk everyday and at every occasion. It's said that chai is stronger than whisky, cheaper than rum, and flows more than vodka…

This is our sideways head wobble to one of my favourite non-alcoholic brews, a little fusion of East and West. Who said they never meet?

chai brew - method

Add two teaspoons of tea per cup to plunger or tea pot. Add one cup hot milk and one cup boiling water and plunge three to four times, or in case of a tea pot - turn 3 times. Steep for three to five minutes depending on how strong you like your brew. Add sweetener to taste and or, add frothed milk for a light milky tea.

pump and pour milk frothing - method

Pour hot frothed milk over half a cup of brewed tea for a latté tea experience. 'Pump & pour' type milk frothers utilize a plunger attached to a circular mesh-type screen that fits inside the plunger. Simply fill the plunger approximately a third full with hot milk, then pump the plunger up and down using short, quick strokes to initiate milk frothing. The result is as good as cappuccino froth.

mumbai jumbo chai - dry

Makes 1 small jar, or approximately 36 drinks

90g / 3oz Lipton Loose Leaf Black Tea

30g / 1oz chai masala, (available from most Asian supermarkets)

30g / 1oz drinking chocolate

30g / 1oz cloves

30g / 1oz star anise

2 tablespoons finely chopped ginger

5 cinnamon quills, roughly broken

1 vanilla been, split and scraped

Add ingredients to a small jar and shake well.

fast mumbai jumbo chai latté

I call this the fast Mumbai latté because firstly and foremostly, we're not on Mumbai time. For those of you who know, this is a very special invention which means waiting a long time for things. I mean a very long time, which means chai should be brewed traditionally for around 20 minutes to half an hour. Now you can enjoy the national drink of India in a flash.

Makes 2 drinks

2 teaspoons dry Mumbai Jumbo Chai tea (see above)

1 cup boiling hot water

1 cup hot milk

brown sugar to taste

cinnamon dusting, to garnish (optional)

Add ingredients to a plunger or teapot and steep for 3-5 minutes. Half-fill pre-warmed small bowls. Froth milk using basic milk frothing method (see page 291) if you'd like a frothy cappuccino-style froth. Add sugar to taste and garnish with optional cinnamon dusting.

chilli choc chai

This is an all-time favourite tea for anyone who likes spicy food. Spicy by nature and warming the body by instant effect, chilli and chocolate make a great match.

Makes 4 drinks
2 bags Lipton Chai Tea
1 tablespoon drinking chocolate
1 jalapeño chilli chopped
400ml / 13½oz boiling hot water
1 teaspoon, maple or honey per bowl
hot frothed milk, to top (see p 291)
cocoa dusting, to garnish
chocolate curls, to garnish (see p 240)

Add ingredients to a plunger or tea pot and steep for 3-5 minutes before half-filling bowls. Add hot frothed milk and sweeten with maple syrup or honey. Garnish with cocoa dusting and chocolate curls.

cherry and date chai - dry

Makes 1 small jar, or approximately 36 drinks
90g / 3oz Lipton Loose Leaf Black Tea
30g / 1oz drinking chocolate
90g / 3oz dried cherries
90g / 3oz dried dates, pitted and chopped
2 vanilla beans, split and scraped then chopped finely

Add ingredients to a small jar and shake well. To make 2 bowls add follow basic methods for chai brew and milk frothing (see p 291). Add sugar to taste.

roasted coconut and mint chai - dry

Makes 1 small jar, or approximately 36 drinks

90g / 3oz Lipton Loose Leaf Black Tea

30g / 1oz drinking chocolate

60g / 2oz coconut, long desiccated

30g / 1oz dried mint

dry-roasted coconut, to garnish

Add ingredients to a small jar and shake well. To make 2 bowls follow basic methods for chai plunger brew and pump and pour milk frothing basic methods (see p 291). Add sugar to taste. Garnish with dry-roasted coconut.

mango, rosemary chai

makes 2 drinks

1 bag Lipton Chai Tea

1 bag Lipton Green Tea with Mango

1 sprig fresh rosemary

1 cup boiling hot water

1 cup hot milk

1 teaspoon brown sugar, to sweeten (optional)

rosemary sprig, to garnish

Add ingredients to a plunger or tea pot and steep for 3-5 minutes before half-filling bowls or cups. Add hot frothed milk and sweeten with sugar to taste. Garnish with sprig of rosemary.

jasmine, vanilla and apricot chai - dry

Makes 1 small jar, or approximately 36 drinks

90g / 3oz Lipton Loose Leaf Green Tea with Jasmine

30g / 1oz drinking chocolate

90g / 3oz dried apricots, chopped

3 vanilla beans, split and scraped, then chopped finely

Add ingredients to a small jar and shake well. To make 2 bowls follow basic methods for chai plunger brew and pump and pour milk frothing basic methods (see p 291). Add sugar to taste.

iced tea

Tea is one of the most satisfying and thirst-quenching drinks to enjoy cold. Not only is it really good for you, providing healthy anti-oxidants to rejuvenate the body, the slow released caffeine from tea is easier on the digestive system. You can often add fresh fruit to replace sugar. My fridge commonly has a jug of iced jasmine or green tea in the fridge door. Sometimes, to be a little experimental I'll give it a little citrus kick, or maybe a buzz with some sparkling water.

iced tea -method

Fill a plunger, carafe or iced tea jug with hot water. Keep dry tea separate in a steeping cage or the gauzed tube many pots have for brewing iced tea. Remove tea after 5-10 minutes and add sugar to taste if desired.

For sparkling iced tea, the tea needs to be steeped for 3-5 minutes in a quarter of the water-filled vessel. So for a 1L / 2 pints jug, add 250ml or 8½oz of boiling water. After steeping, stir in sugar and chill in the fridge. Add sparkling water just before serving.

Iced tea is traditionally served sweet - and of course, with ice in the glass. Using some fruit tea combinations means less sugar can make quite a nice variation. Always taste before serving to ensure it's not too bitter from steeping too long. If it is a little too bitter, remember it can always be sweetened with honey.

chill pill iced tea

Makes 1L / 2 pints, or approximately 4 drinks

3 bags Lipton Chamomile Herbal Infusion

1 lemon, cut into wheels

1 vanilla bean, split and scraped

3 tablespoons sugar

1L / 2 pints boiling hot water

6 fresh lemon wheels, to garnish

ice

Add all ingredients to teapot or jug. Steep for 3-5 minutes, stirring occasionally to help dissolve sugar. Strain tea and remove lemon wheels before chilling. Once chilled serve with ice and garnish with fresh lemon wheels.

rosemary, lychee and honeycomb iced tea

Makes 1L / 2 pints or approximately 4 drinks

3 bags Lipton Flavoured Black Tea Honeycomb

1L / 2 pints boiling hot Ocean Spray White Cranberry juice

6 lychees

1 rosemary sprig

1 lime, juiced

3 tablespoons sugar

ice

Add all ingredients, except lime juice to teapot or jug. Steep for 3-5 minutes, stirring occasionally to help dissolve sugar. Remove tea bags and rosemary and chill. Once chilled add lime juice. Serve with ice.

orange and passionfruit iced tea

Makes 1L / 2 pints or approximately 4 drinks

3 bags Lipton Green Tea with Honey

1 orange, cut into wheels

4 tablespoons sugar

1L / 2 pints boiling hot water

1 orange sliced, to garnish

4 teaspoons passionfruit pulp, to garnish

ice

Add all ingredients, except passionfruit to teapot or jug. Steep for 3-5 minutes, stirring occasionally to help dissolve sugar. Remove tea bags and orange wheels before chilling. Serve with ice and garnish with fresh orange wheels and passionfruit pulp.

rosemary and peach iced tea

Makes 1L / 2 pints or approximately 4 drinks

3 bags Lipton Green Tea with Honey

2 sprigs fresh rosemary

1 peach, cut into slice

1 lime, juiced

4 tablespoons sugar

1L / 2 pints boiling hot water

ice

Add all ingredients to teapot or jug. Steep for 3-5 minutes, stirring occasionally to help dissolve sugar. Remove tea before chilling. Serve with ice and garnish with fresh peach slice.

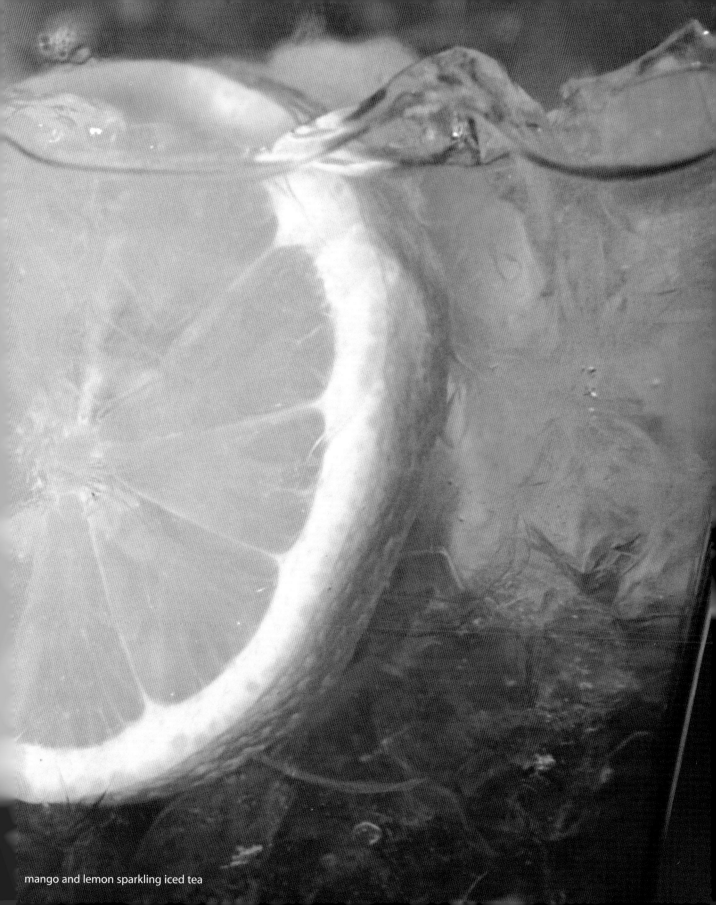

mango and lemon sparkling iced tea

mango and lemon sparkling iced tea

Makes 1L / 2 pints or approximately 6 drinks

3 bags Lipton Green Tea with Lemon

½ green mango, chopped into big chunks

2 lemons, juiced

60ml maple syrup

250ml / 8½oz boiling hot water

750ml / 25oz sparkling water

6 mango slices, to garnish

6 lemon wheels, to garnish

ice

Add all ingredients to teapot or jug. Steep for 3-5 minutes, stirring occasionally to help dissolve sugar. Remove tea bags before chilling. Once chilled add sparkling water with ice. Garnish with fresh mango slices and lemon wheels.

jasmine and lemon sparkling iced tea

Makes 1L / 2 pints or approximately 6 drinks

2 bags Lipton Green Tea with Jasmine

1 bag Lipton Lemon Herbal Infusion

1 lemon, cut into wheels

1 lemon, juiced

4 tablespoons sugar

250ml / 8½oz boiling hot water

750ml / 125oz sparkling water

6 lemon wheels, to garnish

6 lemongrass ice cubes, to garnish

ice

Add all ingredients, except lemon juice to teapot or jug. Steep for 3-5 minutes, stirring occasionally to help dissolve sugar. Remove tea bags before chilling. Once chilled add lemon juice and sparkling water and serve with ice. Garnish with fresh lemon wheels and lemongrass ice cubes.

To make lemongrass ice cubes simply place sliced lemongrass into ice tray with water before freezing.

lychee, mint and apple sparkling iced tea

Makes 1L / 2 pints or approximately 6 drinks

3 bags Lipton Green Tea with Jasmine

5 lychees, whole

2 mint sprigs

2 limes, juiced

4 tablespoons sugar

250ml / 8½oz boiling hot water

750ml / 25oz sparkling water

fresh lime rind, to garnish

fresh mint, to garnish

Add all ingredients except lime juice to teapot or jug. Steep for 3-5 minutes, stirring occasionally to help dissolve sugar. Remove tea bags before chilling. Once chilled add lime juice, sparkling water and ice. Garnish with fresh lime rind and mint. See page 26 for more on citrus rind.

ginger bite sparkling iced tea

Makes 1L / 2pints or approximately 4 drinks

3 bags Lipton Green Tea with Honey

2 tablespoons ginger, finely chopped

1 lime, cut into wheels

1 lime, juiced

4 tablespoons sugar

250ml / 8½oz boiling hot water

750ml / 25oz sparkling water

2 limes cut into wheels, to garnish

Add all ingredients, except lime juice to teapot or jug. Steep for 3-5 minutes, stirring occasionally to help dissolve sugar. Remove tea bags and lime wheels before chilling. Once chilled add lime juice and sparkling water and serve with ice. Garnish with fresh lime wheels.

ultra cool waters

I wanted to share a great idea for mixing lightly-flavoured water. I used to do this often to disguise the tainted flavour water can have after sitting in old pipes or chemical treatments like chlorination or fluoridation. It's probably the reason many people don't like drinking much water, even when all the available scientific and medical evidence suggests that drinking plenty of water - at least two litres (or eight glasses) each day is essential to good health. I've tried to make water fun and taste good too - and you'll enjoy my favourites like Basil and Blueberry on page 312 or Soda Lime and Bitters on page 320, to ensure you're always guzzling your daily quota!

Mixing alcohol-free drinks like juices, mocktails or flavoured waters are a fun way of keeping you practising your drinks-mixing skills. They're also a great way to ensure that the poor old designated driver or teetotaller isn't lumped with OJ or plain water. Experimenting with different juice and flavour combinations, you may well find a new recipe in there somewhere - and unlike the cocktail recipes in the rest of the book, you don't have to wait till the cocktail hour to try!

Using an old jug from a second-hand store and adding different leftovers from home or the bar, I soon discovered my very necessary invention went extremely well with carbonated water as well.

For those who don't drink enough water each day -
2L / 4 pints or 8 glasses a day is your target.

This infused water idea could be for you. You'll enjoy the flavour more, you'll be inspired to drink more as you've spent the time making it and, if all else fails, you'll probably drink it in fear of wasting the infusing ingredients.

basil and blueberry water

At my own cocktail events, I often keep a big jug of basil and blueberry water on the bar for guests to help themselves. Sometimes people don't feel comfortable asking for - or think it's their place to ask - for water at a party. But keeping freely available and palatable water on the bar or a table, ensures that guests can quench the thirst that comes with drinking, without resorting to another alcoholic drink. It's also an attractive looking drink that ensures more people will drink some, rather than resorting to the kitchen tap - or not drinking any water at all!

Makes 2L or 4 pints, or approximately 8 drinks
1 handful fresh basil
½ cup blueberries
2L / 4 pints water
ice

Build ingredients over ice in a large jug.

kaffir and rose water

This is a great water to serve with High Tea. Cool and refreshing, it's also quite exotic, reminiscent of lazy tropical afternoons in deep rattan chairs... Be sure to wash rose petals thoroughly to remove herbicides or pesticides.

Makes 2L or 4 pints, or approximately 8 drinks
10-12 fresh kaffir lime leaves
2 teaspoons rosewater
2L / 4 pints water
20-30 rose petals, to garnish
ice

Build ingredients over ice in a large jug.

vanilla, honey and strawberry water

Makes 2L or 4 pints, or approximately 8 drinks

10 strawberries, sliced

1 vanilla bean, split and scraped

2 tablespoons honey

2L / 4 pints water

ice

Build ingredients over ice in a large jug.

blood orange and ginger water

Makes 2L or 4 pints, or approximately 8 drinks

1 large knob ginger, sliced finely

1 blood orange wheels, thinly sliced

2L / 4 pints water

ice

Build ingredients over ice in a large jug.

peach and lime water

When I first moved out of home I lived in a crumbling tenement, sleeping on the floor of a shoebox that was always covered in mates recovering from nasty hangovers and that peculiarly distinctive smell that young men are well known for: jocks, socks and... well, you get the idea. The water that sputtered desultorily from the kitchen tap didn't taste much better than the smell of the room, and so a little flavour enhancer was much needed. Here's a classic example of the kind of recipe that I used to disguise the water I used to drink.

Makes 2L or 4 pints, or approximately 8 drinks

2 limes, sliced into wheels

1 peach, pitted and finely sliced

1L / 2 pints Ocean Spray White Cranberry Peach juice

1L / 2 pints water

ice

Build ingredients over ice in a large jug.

refresh water

Makes 2L or 4 pints, or approximately 8 drinks

1 cup table grapes

1 handful fresh mint

2 mandarins, sliced into wheels

2L / 4 pints water

ice

Build ingredients over ice in a large jug.

refresh water

yo-yo sparkling water

I call this the yo-yo because of the effect of the sparkling water on the tamarillo, which causes the fruit to rise and fall in the jug, up and down, up and down. Tamarillo's taste like slightly tangy with a later sweetness of tomatoes crossed with rock melon. Be warned, it might take some time before you drink it with all the yoyo action going on. But you'll have fun! And it tastes as good as it looks too.

Makes 2L or 4 pints, or approximately 8 drinks
1 tamarillo, cut into wheels
1 orange, chopped julienne
2 tablespoons maple syrup
2L / 4 pints sparkling water
ice

Build ingredients over ice in a large jug. Stir maple syrup through water before serving.

soda, lime and bitters

More thirst-quenching than the usual lemon, lime and bitters, this is a supercharged twist on one of the world's most popular low-alcohol drinks. Low alcohol? I hear you say. Well, Angostura bitters is actually 44.7% alcohol by volume, similar in strength to some whiskeys! And although 7 - 8 dashes is more than the average 1 - 2 dashes in most LLBs (lemonade lime and bitters), it won't push anyone over the limit - alcoholically, anyway. But it is a much more exciting drink!

Makes 1 drink
7-8 dashes Angostura bitters
60ml / 2oz lime cordial
soda water, to top
2 lime wedges, squeezed
ice

Add Angostura bitters to inside of highball glass, spinning glass so inside is lined with bitters. This not only helps spread Angostura bitters through the drink, it's also the professional way of mixing it. Build remaining ingredients over ice in glass.

woody lines the glass with a spin

lime and pear sparkling

Makes 2L or 4 pints, or approximately 8 drinks

1 pear, chopped julienne

1 lime sliced into wheels

2 tablespoons liquid honey

2L / 4 pints sparkling water

ice

Build ingredients over ice in a large jug. Stir through honey before serving.

plum and passionfruit sparkling

Makes 2L or 4 pints, or approximately 8 drinks

3 passionfruit, halved and squeezed

1 plum, sliced into wheels

2 tablespoons liquid honey

2L / 4 pints sparkling water

ice

Build ingredients over ice in a large jug. Stir honey through water before serving.

cinnamon and strawberry sparkling water

Makes 2L or 4 pints, or approximately 8 drinks

½ cup strawberries

5 cinnamon quills

2 tablespoons liquid honey

2L / 4 pints sparkling water

ice

Build ingredients over ice in a large jug. Stir through honey before serving.

lemon, boysenberry and mint sparkling water

Makes 2L or 4 pints, or approximately 8 drinks

½ cup boysenberries

3 sprigs mint

½ cup lemon juice

60ml / 2oz liquid honey

2L / 4 pints sparkling water

ice

Dissolve lemon and sugar before adding berries, mint and sparkling water to a large jug. Stir honey through water before serving.

honeydew and rosemary sparkling water

Makes 2L or 4 pints, or approximately 8 drinks

¼ honeydew melon, chopped into chunks

2 sprigs fresh rosemary, with stalks

2 tablespoons liquid honey

2L / 4 pints sparkling water

ice

Build ingredients over ice in a large jug. Stir through honey before serving.

cambodian lemonade

Served throughout South-East-Asia, I first tried this drink in Phnom Penh, the capital of Cambodia. I'd heard about it from all the travellers we met. They swore that a glass a day would keep the doctor - and heat exhaustion - away. Even in tropical Cambodia, it was the hottest part of the year and although it was only about 40 degrees centigrade, the humidity made everyone sweat like demons. Drinking this lemonade with salt replenished what I relentlessly sweated out. A very tasty splash of the east in the west.

Makes 2L or 4 pints, or approximately 8 drinks
1 cup of freshly squeezed lemon juice
2 cups sugar
2 teaspoons salt
2L / 4 pints sparkling water
fresh Cambodian mint sprig, to garnish
ice

Dissolve lemon, salt and sugar before adding sparkling water to a large jug. Garnish with fresh mint sprig.

The Cambodian mint used in this drink is now available in some specialist provedores. It's almost a cross between a thinner, narrower kaffir lime leaf and mint. It's very peppery and more robust in flavour. If you can't find it, common fresh mint will do.

twenty-five classic cocktails

Okay, all you 'die hard with a vengeance' cocktail makers and shakers. I'll keep you happy with some of the world's most popular cocktails. From the Savoy Hotel in London, or Harry's Bar in Venice, to the Red Car Bar and Grill in LA, these drinks have wet the whistles of millions of happy drinkers the world over.

I've seen these drinks on cocktail menus right around the world - even in the remote and impoverished capital of Cambodia, Phnom Penh. While staying at the grand old La Cambodian hotel and drinking with shady American prospectors, we all agreed it was quite astonishing to find a bar in deepest darkest South East Asia that could shake up a good martini - or in my case, a Mienekin.

For those of you who are wondering what the ingredients of my all time classic favourites are, it's simple - a good Margarita in one hand and a Heineken in the other. I alternate between drinks and eventually… well, you get the picture. I got everyone in that wonderful old bar hooked on Mienekens. Remember that old Coke ad? I wish I could give everyone in the world a Coke? Well, I wish I could give everyone in the world a Mienekin.

And besides, I'm a lot more attractive and witty when everyone's drinking Mienekins. Okay, to myself, at least. Think of them as potent and very drinkable beer goggles.

It doesn't matter where you are in the world, whether you're behind the bar or in your kitchen. You can always enjoy some of the world's favourite cocktails. Chin-chin!

alexander

Most seasoned cocktail drinkers would be familiar with a brandy alexander cocktail. The difference is simply the substitution of gin for brandy. Although gin is the original spirit base for this cocktail, the brandy version has gained a greater popularity because of its warm flavours that go well with the crème de cacao or chocolate liqueur.

Makes 1 drink
30ml / 1oz South gin
30ml / 1oz crème de cacao dark
30ml / 1oz cream
nutmeg dusting, to garnish (see p 36)
ice

Shake and strain all ingredients into chilled martini glass. Garnish with a dusting of nutmeg.

americano highball

This is the grand-daddy of most modern cocktails. Most popular mixed drinks, like the bourbon and dry or vodka and tonic, all trace their lineage to the Americano Highball. It's not simply its flavour that made it so popular, but its simplicity. Ingredients are poured over ice in a highball glass, so named because it's reminiscent of the 'high balls' on poles that warned drivers that their locomotive was running late on the old American railways. Hence the Americano Highball: a quick, easy drink to make in the flash of a highball.

Makes 1 drink
30ml / 1oz Campari
60ml / 2oz sweet vermouth (Rosso)
sparkling water, to top
lemon rind, to garnish
ice

Build and stir in a highball glass. Garnish with lemon rind.

bloody mary

As a bartender, I've heard thousands of 'sure-fire' hangover cures. Raw eggs, pickled herrings… even the old voodoo trick of sticking thirteen pins in the cork of the offending bottle (although, if you're like me, you might run out of bottles). You name it, I've heard it. But apart from a Berocca and a bacon sandwich, the original and best remedy is the bloody mary, named after the infamous Queen Mary of England, who persecuted and killed Protestants throughout the land before her younger sister Elizabeth I acceded to the throne.

Although many people don't find tomato juice appealing, this invigorating juice - often found as an aperitif in good restaurants around the world - has many variations to please almost everyone. Packed with vitamin C (in the tomato juice, lime and Tabasco) it replenishes your poor dehydrated body whilst numbing the pain somewhat with the hair of the dog (that bitchya). The chilli acts as a sort of diversion, stimulating saliva production and taking your mind off your headache!

Makes 1 drink
60ml / 2oz 42 Below vodka
60ml / 2oz tomato juice
15ml / ½oz Worcestershire sauce
½ teaspoon horseradish
5 drops dry sherry
3-5 drops Tabasco sauce
1 lime wedge squeezed
pinch salt
pinch caster sugar
cracked pepper and celery stick, to garnish
ice

Shake and strain into an ice-filled highball glass. Garnish with cracked pepper and celery stick.

caipiriñha

Traditionally, this tangy and refreshing taste sensation is made with cachaça, a Brazilian white spirit similar to rum. It's a stauncher spirit, stronger to taste than smooth rum. Although it works well with the sweet and sour mash of limes and sugar, I prefer light or white rum - which are also a lot easier to find! Consider using palm sugar or any of the other sugars listed in the Methods and Hip Things chapter on page 19 in place of caster sugar, for that convincingly tropical taste.

Makes 1 drink

60ml / 2oz Havana Club Añejo Blanco rum

½ glass fresh limes, chopped with skins left on

20ml / ¾oz sugar syrup (see p 21)

3 teaspoons caster sugar

ice

Muddle limes and sugar in base of mixing glass. Add remaining ingredients then shake and pour unstrained into an old-fashioned glass. For more on muddling see page 30.

caipiroska

A derivative of the Caipiriñha, it's a result from the growing popularity of vodka, and a good one at that. Most people find it hard to turn down a good Caipiroska, even if they have difficulty pronouncing it. But hey, if someone asks for a Capriciosa (which is actually a pizza) they might be asking for this, especially if they're in a bar and not a pizza joint!

Makes 1 drink

60ml / 2oz 42 Below vodka

½ glass fresh limes, chopped with skins left on

20ml / ¾oz sugar syrup (see p 21)

3 teaspoons caster sugar

ice

Muddle limes and sugar in base of mixing glass. Add remaining ingredients then shake and pour unstrained into an old-fashioned glass. For more on muddling see page 30.

cape cod

Named after the Cape Cod in Massachusetts, USA, where a great deal of cranberry juice is produced.

Makes 1 drink

45ml / 1½oz 42 Below vodka

120ml / 4oz Ocean Spray Cranberry Classic juice

lime squeeze, to garnish

ice

Build over ice in highball glass. Garnish with lime squeeze.

cosmopolitan

Made global by the popularity of Sex and the City, the Cosmopolitan is now hailed as a modern day classic. By definition, a classic cocktail is a mixed drink that you can ask for by name which will be served without hesitation. It needs to be a relatively simple drink with readily available products, and the Cosmo has all that going for it. Plus, the cranberry juice is particularly good for women - hence its popularity.

Makes 1 drink

45ml / 1½oz 42 Below vodka

15ml / ½oz Grand Marnier (curaçao orange liqueur or Chambord as substitutes)

30ml / 1oz sweet 'n' sour mix (see p 40)

60ml / 2oz Ocean Spray Cranberry Classic juice

lime wedge, to garnish

ice

Shake and strain all ingredients into a chilled martini or cocktail glass. Garnish with lime wedge on rim of glass.

daiquiri

Hailing from Port Daiquiri in Cuba around 150 years ago, this old favourite is said to have been invented by two sailors who were rationed a quota of limes to eat each day to prevent scurvy, a horrible vitamin deficiency that results in black gums and loose teeth - hence so many toothless pirates... aaaarrrrgh (doesn't explain the peg legs and eye patches, though).

Having no palate for fresh limes eaten on their own, the inventive sailors sweetened it with a little sugar. Of course, a little rum was never far away - and the rest is history.

Makes 1 drink
45ml / 1 ½oz Havana Club Añejo Blanco rum
15ml / ½oz Grand Marnier
60ml / 2oz sweet 'n' sour mix (see p 40)
lime wedge, to garnish
ice

Shake and strain all ingredients into a chilled martini or cocktail glass. Garnish with lime wedge on rim of glass. Alternately a Daiquiri can be served over ice in an old-fashioned glass. Although I don't think the sailors were all too fussed about their glassware and you needn't be either.

golden cadillac

Makes 1 drink
30ml / 1oz Galliano Vanilla
30ml / 1oz white crème de cacao liqueur
90ml / 3oz half 'n' half (see p 41)
crushed ice

Blend all ingredients and pour in a chilled wine or cocktail glass.

golden dream

Makes 1 drink

30ml / 1oz Galliano Vanilla

30ml / 1oz Grand Marnier

60ml / 2oz half 'n' half (see p 41)

30ml / 1oz fresh freshly juiced orange juice

ice

Shake and strain into a chilled martini glass. See page 30 for more on shaking and straining.

harvey wallbanger

The story goes that there was a gnarly surfer called Harvey. He caught several bodacious waves off the coast of California on a hot summer's day back in the early Seventies. While visiting his local bar, to celebrate his bitchin' adventure, he added a long bottle of Galliano on top off his usual Screw Driver (or vodka and orange juice). After a few of these very drinkable cocktails, he ended up bouncing off every wall in the bar while attempting his exit. Or so the story goes…

Makes 1 drink

60ml / 2oz 42 Below vodka

15ml / ½oz Galliano Vanilla, to float

90ml / 3oz fresh freshly juiced orange juice

orange slice and a maraschino cherry, to garnish

ice

Build over ice in highball glass. Float the Galliano liqueur on top of the freshly juiced orange juice. To float Galliano, pour as the last ingredient, slowly over vodka and orange juice.

The garnish is usually pinned together with a toothpick. In a cocktail bar this is refereed to a 'flag garnish'. Naming prepared garnishes that consist of more than one fruit save long descriptions, especially when the bar's packed six deep. Saying 'pass the flag garnishes please' in place of 'the-cherries-pinned-to-orange-slices-with-toothpicks-please' saves time when calling for them, but it's a very 'bar' thing to do.

japanese slipper

Made in the same way as a Sour, see page 346, but created a generation or two afterwards, the Japanese Slipper gets its name from the internationally famous Midori cocktail competition. Bartenders are asked to create cocktail recipes and mix them in front of a judging panel. They are marked on their ability to mix it, its presentation, flavour... and even the name of the drink! With a flavour that most connoisseurs find appealing, the Japanese Slipper - a little like Cinderella's slipper, perhaps - has turned many drinking nights into fairytales.

Makes 1 drink
30ml / 1oz Midori
30ml / 1oz curaçao orange liqueur (Grand Marnier optional)
90ml / 3oz sweet 'n' sour mix (see p 40)
sugar rim, to garnish (optional) (see p 26)
ice

Shake and strain into a chilled martini glass. Garnishing with sugar rim is optional. As this drink was created when sweet 'n' sour mix wasn't popular, the original used fresh lime juice. To balance the resultant tartness, a sugar rim was used. To make this a little more suitable to most people's taste, I prefer to use sweet 'n' sour mix, rendering the sugar rim optional. It's up to you.

john collins

Using very simple ingredients and an easy method, the John Collins also gained popularity with other variations. Replacing bourbon with vodka to make a Joan Collins or gin to mix a Jack Collins.

60ml / 2oz bourbon
60ml / 2oz lemon juice
2 teaspoons caster sugar
soda water, to top
ice

Build over ice in a highball glass in stir until sugar is dissolved.

knickerbocker special

The Knickerbocker Special was the signature cocktail at Rumours, the great 70s London club, which was a sister club to the infamous Studio 54 in New York. You can only imagine who drank one and what they were doing when they were drinking it…

Makes 1 drink
45ml / 1½oz Havana Club Añejo Blanco rum
15ml / ½oz Grand Marnier
15ml / ½oz lemon juice
15ml / ½oz fresh orange juice
30ml / 1oz pineapple juice
10ml / ¼oz raspberry cordial
ice

Shake and strain into a chilled cocktail glass.

long island iced tea

Long Island, upstate New York, is famous for working-class Brooklyn and the Bronx at its south end, and the more rarefied air of the Hamptons, where Manhattan's rich and famous like to play. The Hamptons have been a luxurious getaway for generations, and during the Great Gatsby's time, lazy flappers would sip away on the Long Island Iced Tea as they danced the Charleston. While many think it's a quick way to empty the liquor cabinet into a highball glass, it's actually quite a well-balanced drink, which adheres to the Golden Rule of Cocktails, which is that ninety-five percent of cocktails are made of; 60ml or 2oz spirit or liqueur mixed with 90ml or 3oz alcohol-free ingredients such as fruit juice, mixers, sweeteners or soft drink.

Although some recent variations also include tequila, using sweet 'n' sour mix makes it redundant. With less bitterness, less cola can be used.

Most people build this drink. However, there is some advantage to shaking and straining the ingredients, except the cola, into an ice-filled cocktail glass. By mixing spirits and mixers thoroughly, there's no nasty hot alcohol surprises for the unsuspecting drinker at the bottom of the glass.

Makes 1 drink
15ml / ½oz 42 Below vodka
15ml / ½oz South gin
15ml / ½oz Havana Club Añejo Blanco rum
15ml / ½oz Grand Marnier
60ml / 2oz sweet 'n' sour mix (see p 40)
30ml / 1oz cola, or top with
lemon wedge, to garnish
ice

Shake and strain all ingredients except cola into an ice-filled cocktail glass. Top with cola, staining drink to appear the colour of iced tea.

margarita

Although there's many variations of the way a Margarita can be served: sweet, sour, frozen, blended or without ice. Yet the basic ingredients largely remain the same.

The famous actor Sam Neil likes his Margaritas the all-time classic way, shaken and strained, salt rim, served up (without ice) in a margarita glass. But he sometimes takes a shot of tequila on the side.

Makes 1 drink

45ml / 1½oz Cuervo tequila

15ml / ½oz Grand Marnier

60ml / 2oz sweet 'n' sour mix (see p 40)

squeezed lime wedge, to garnish

salted rim, to garnish

ice

When someone asks for a Margarita, you should take note of their mixing instructions. Some of the ways it can be served include:

- Shaken and strained into a chilled, salt rimmed margarita glass. A margarita glass is like a martini glass, but more curvaceous with a bulbous cup at the top of the stem. See page 30 for more on shaking and straining.
- Shaken and strained into an ice-filled, salt rimmed old-fashioned glass or goblet. See page 25 for more on rimming.
- Blended with ice. As blended drinks are often served with straws for ease of drinking, it's sometimes not necessary to salt the rim of the glass. See page 35 for more on blending.

A good thing to note is that the basic recipe for a Margarita is also the basic recipe for a Daiquiri, a Kamikaze and a Side Car. The difference is simply changing the basic spirit base. So a good rule to remember is:

Vodka = Kamikaze

Rum = Daiquiri

Cognac = Side Car

See? Now you know four classic cocktails! Easy, isn't it?

midori splice

Just as the Piña Colada, see page 345, mixes coconut milk with pineapple juice, the Midori Splice combines two of my favourites, the melon of Midori and the coconut of Malibu, to very sultry effect.

Makes 1 drink
30ml / 1oz Midori
30ml / 1oz Malibu
60ml / 2oz pineapple juice
30ml / 1oz fresh cream, top float

In a cocktail glass, preferably a stemmed tulip glass (also known as a poco grandé), build ingredients over ice. Float cream on top of pineapple by slowly pouring it over a spoon placed on the surface of the glass. This will assist with a cleaner separation, although moments later, you must plunge a couple of straws through it and mix it together before sipping and relaxing by the pool.

mimosa

45ml / 1 ½oz fresh orange juice
Piper-Heidseick champagne, to top

Build in a chilled champagne flute with out ice.

mojito

The national drink of Cuba, the Mojito was one of the first drinks to popularise muddling (see page 30). Using the freshest ingredients and best quality rum yields a drink full of vigour and flavour. Fresh mint bursts through the sweetness, balanced by the refreshing zing of lime. An often overlooked ingredient in a truly traditional Mojito is Angostura bitters. A few dashes on top and this great drinks takes on a whole new character. Although you may get a strange look from a busy barman if you ask for Angostura bitters, the knowledgeable ones will know. And hey - don't be discouraged, it's your drink anyway! Viva la revolucion!

Makes 1 drink
60ml / 2oz Havana Club Añejo Blanco rum
½ glass fresh limes, chopped with skins left on
5-10 fresh mint leaves
20ml / ¾oz sugar syrup (see p 21)
3 teaspoons caster sugar
sparkling water, to top
Angostura bitters, to top (optional)
ice

Muddle limes, mint and sugars in base of mixing glass. Add rum and ice then shake and pour unstrained into highball glass. Top with sparkling water followed by Angostura bitters.

negroni

Makes 1 drink
20ml / ¾oz South gin
20ml / ¾oz sweet vermouth (Rosso)
20ml / ¾oz Campari
sparkling water, to top
orange zest, to garnish
ice

Build and stir in an ice-filled old-fashioned glass. Garnish with orange zest.

old fashioned cocktail

Like other classic cocktails such as the Martini or the Margarita, the Old Fashioned is deemed worthy enough of its own eponymous glass. Although once drunk by the staunch bourbon drinker, these days the Old Fashioned has been overtaken by the much simpler - and less elegant - bourbon and coke. While it takes a little more time to make, this is a great drink, full of complex subtleties and very, very drinkable.

Makes 1 drink

90ml / 3oz sweet bourbon

3-4 teaspoons caster sugar

3-4 dashes Angostura bitters

1 large orange zest

1 large orange zest, to garnish

1 maraschino cherry, to garnish (optional)

ice

Twist one orange zest to release oils into old-fashioned glass. Add half the sugar and bitters and stir together. After stirring in bursts of 10-12 revolutions at a time, add bourbon in pours of around 20ml / ¾oz. Add a little more sugar, then stir again. Continue this until all ingredients have been used or desired taste has been achieved.

Bruising orange zest during the long stirring process will result in a more pungent orange flavour. The optional maraschino cherry is, as they say, the cherry on the top - but in this case, it's actually in the bottom of the glass. Garnish with more orange zest.

piña colada

There have been many songs about this all-time classic: Two Piña Coladas, Piña Colada Morning, Piña Colada Love Song, and of course, Escape (The Piña Colada Song) by Rupert Holmes. Remember him? Me neither. But who can forget the effect of a couple too many drinks, the end of the night, the stereo blaring out *Do you like Piña Coladas? Getting caught in the rain? Are you not into yoga? Do you like drinking champagne?* To which I'd say 'Yes, no, maybe... and of course.'

There are so many recipes for this big, fruity, creamy combination of pineapple and coconut. In previous books, I've used Piña Colada recipes for large batches of drinks with a base mix (see page 40 for more on mixers). This is a great, simple recipe for keeping the party going all night long.

Makes 1 drink
45ml / 1½oz Havana Club Añejo Blanco rum
30ml / 1oz pineapple juice
30ml / 1oz mango nectar
20ml / ¾oz coconut milk
20ml / ¾oz sugar syrup (see p 21)
desiccated coconut rim, to garnish (see p 25)
pineapple leaf, to garnish (optional)
ice

Shake and strain all ingredients into ice-filled cocktail glass. A hurricane or tall tulip shaped glass is mostly suited to this cocktail. But if you're more about flavour than presentation, pour it up into any kind of glass. Why not try Piña Colada shaker shots. Pour cocktail from shaker into a shot glass for each person at the party. Hula hoops aside for a moment, let the colada slide down and the limbo go a little lower. Salud!

sour

A Sour is a little like a Daiquiri or a Margarita, except it doesn't include a curaçao (orange) flavoured liqueur. It's sourer by nature and popular varieties include bourbon whisky for a Whisky Sour, because bourbon's usually sweeter than Scotch whisky. The Amaretto Sour comes a close second in popularity. One of the desired attributes of a Sour (whether Amaretto or Bourbon) is that although it has a tart, acidic taste, it should also be light and fluffy in texture. This is achieved by shaking egg white with the other ingredients. If you wish, you can substitute powdered egg white and use a caster sugar rim, if you prefer it a little less sour.

Makes 1 drink
45ml / 1½oz desired spirit or liqueur
60ml / 2oz fresh lemon juice
½ fresh egg white (powdered egg white can be substituted)
2 teaspoons caster sugar
caster sugar rim, to garnish (option for less sour taste)
ice

Shake and strain all ingredients into a small chilled martini glass. Garnish with caster sugar rim. Alternatively, shake and strain into an ice-filled old-fashioned glass. This is a more masculine look and, using bourbon, can be a sure way of getting a male drinker to try a cocktail.

spencer cocktail

45ml / 1½oz South gin
15ml / ½oz apricot brandy
1 dash Angostura bitters
30ml / 1oz orange juice
maraschino cherry, to garnish
ice

Shake and strain into a chilled cocktail glass. Garnish with a maraschino cherry.

zombie

Commonly referred to as the loco party drink because of its high rum content, the zombie can have the effect to bring people back from the dead with one mouthful.

Makes 1 drink

30ml / 1oz Havana Club Añejo Blanco rum

30ml / 1oz Havana Club Añejo Reserva rum

30ml / 1oz Havana Club Añejo 7 Años

2 dashes Angostura bitters

30ml / 1oz pineapple juice

30ml / 1oz lime juice

pineapple wedge, to garnish

pineapple leaves, to garnish

ice

Shake and strain all ingredients into an ice filled cocktail glass. Garnish with pineapple wedge and pineapple leaves.

glossary

terminology

boston cocktail shaker

This is a two piece shaker consisting of a mixing glass and a cocktail shaker 'can' or 'tin'. When fitted together they form a boston cocktail shaker. For more on boston cocktail shaker see page 28.

build

Building a drink is, by and large, the most simple method for making a drink. Pour the listed ingredients over ice in the desired glass.

chilled glass

Refers to a cold glass without ice. Glasses can be chilled by placing them in the fridge if you have enough space. They can also have ice placed in them while you are mixing the drink, remembering to discard ice before pouring drink.

crushed ice

Crushed ice is normally added to glasses - and sometimes a blender - when preparing drinks. It is almost impossible to buy, so to make it by wrapping a scoop of ice in a clean tea towel, then bashing it with a rolling pin until crushed. Very cathartic!

hawthorne strainer

A metal strainer that fits over the end of a mixing glass or cocktail shaker. It has a special coil, which when fitted and a drink is poured through, strains most of the solid ingredients.

ice

Where ice is referred to in a recipe, it can be added to the cocktail shaker and then strained. Where it is listed as an ice-filled glass, the recipe may call for the ice to be added to the cocktail shaker and the glass. Ice listed at the bottom of a recipe means that ice will be required in the drink.

ice-filled glass

Refers to a glass filled with ice. Always use lots of ice in drinks. This will keep the drink colder for longer and slow the dilution of ingredients. If your drinks are tasting watery then consider adding more ice.

jigger or measure

A small double ended measuring cup commonly referred to in bars as a jigger. Although various size combinations are available an example is 30ml / 1oz on one end and 15ml / ½oz on the other. Pour liquid into the jigger and then from the jigger into mixing glass or blender. A sneaky option is to use the measuring cup in the lid of a Sunbeam blender. It can measure from 30 - 60ml.

juice

Referring to bottled or packaged juice. The advantage in using bottled premium juices like the Ocean Spray range is that they are 'long life' juices providing a convenient storage and resealable product. Once opened keep refrigerated and the juice will last with the same freshness for a week.

juicing or juiced

Referring to juicing fresh ingredients in a juicer machine like the Sunbeam juicer. Fresh ingredients are pushed into the machine and the seeds, skins and stalks are separated leaving fresh serve of juice.

layer

Layering, by pouring liquor over the back of a spoon, can give your drinks a special look. Pour slowly and keep a steady hand, remembering to select the order of your liquor before you commence layering, as some products will be denser than others.

mixing spoon

A long spoon to plunge through ice in a mixing glass and stir the ingredients. It can also be used for layering ingredients on top of one another. A mixing spoon is sometimes referred to as a bar spoon.

muddling pin or muddling stick

Used for muddling or crushing fruits and other ingredients in the base of a mixing glass. A French rolling pin will work well, as will many other rolling pins. Watch out as some mums don't like the ends of their rolling pins stained with berries! Best to buy one from a kitchen supply store.

pour spout

Pour spouts are usually made with a plastic or metal pourer and rubber cork. Fitter together the unit sits in the neck of the bottle with a tight fit so as not to come out when pouring. It will control the flow of the liquid and allow a more consistent pour. In some bars, bartenders will be able to pour using a pour spout and calculate the amount of liquor poured - this is called free pouring.

glassware

champagne glasses

Come in two different shapes. The most common is the champagne flute, a tall, narrow glass with a tulip shaped bowl on a long stem for drinking... champagne! The other, less fashionable glass is the champagne saucer, so named because of its wide, flat bowl. With a similar stem to a wine glass, it's said the current 'coupe' shape was modelled on Marie-Antoinette's breasts. While popular in the past, connoisseurs tend to avoid its flat shape as it allows rapid dissolution of the bubbles.

cocktail glass

The term 'cocktail glass' is varied and wide. And in terms of choice, when listed as the glass in the method of a recipe, use anything a little fancier than a plain highball or old-fashioned glass. Consider stemmed glasses of with interesting shapes and unusual colours or textures. Look for funky or bizarre cocktail glasses in second hand shops, flea markets and antique stores.

highball glass

A tall glass with straight or slightly angled sides. With a heavy base, the highball glass is one of the most common glasses in the world.

martini glass

Synonymous with style and class the world over, the martini glass has a long stem supporting an elegant funnel-shaped bowl. A popular iconic piece of glassware.

milk bar cup

A metal cup that looks a lot like a cocktail shaker, except that it's wider and more robust. These are the traditional metal cups in which shakes are served in milk bars and cafés.

old-fashioned glass

A short tumbler, similar in shape to a highball glass.

shot glass

Commonly a 30ml / 1oz small glass. Also known as a whiskey glass and can also come in 60ml / 2oz.

spirits and liqueurs

amaretto
A sweet almond liqueur.

angostura bitters
A bitter spiced and herbal spirit used in many food dishes and drink recipes around the world.

bourbon whiskey
Comes from Bourbon County in Kentucky state USA. Bourbon is a whiskey made with 51% corn, aged in American oak barrels.

campari
A dry orange-flavoured aperitif from Italy.

cognac
Brandy that is produced in the Cognac region of France. Remy Martin Grand Cru is the cognac used in this book as it's a smooth, aged spirit that's very drinkable and very affordable.

crème de cacao (white or dark)
A sweet chocolate liqueur. The dark is the colour of cocoa whereas the white is actually clear.

curaçao
An orange liqueur made from curaçao oranges, which are found mainly in the Caribbean. Where curaçao is listed, you may consider Grand Marnier as a more premium alternative.

espresso coffee
Coffee that has been drawn from an espresso coffee machine. See page 246 for more on espresso and a look at my choice of home coffee making using the great Sunbeam machine.

framboise
A rich sweet berry liqueur made with a combination of berries including Framboise berries.

frangelico

A sweet hazelnut liqueur from Italy.

galliano

A predominantly vanilla but with a slight herbal aftertaste, Galliano can often be confused with Galliano sambuca which has a strong anise flavour. Where Galliano is listed in a recipe, it refers to the gold coloured vanilla liqueur.

gin

A herbal and floral white spirit made with the infusion of botanicals, especially the juniper berry. However, in the case of South gin from New Zealand, many native Kiwi herbs have been added to give it a unique character.

grand marnier

An orange-flavoured, brandy-based liqueur from France. Used in cocktails around the world, it's famous for its rich and slightly caramel orange taste.

midori

A vibrant green melon liqueur from Mexico. Famous for its popularity as a sweetener in sour drinks like the Japanese Slipper.

rum

Made from fermented sugar cane, then distilled and in some cases (like Havana Club Añejo Reserve rum) aged for years in oak barrels. The result is a smooth, warming spirit with the essence of Cuba.

sambuca

A liquorice-flavoured liqueur made with both star anise from China and European seed anise. Its often strong alcohol content and addictive flavour have made Sambuca popular with shots or shooters. A short drink that, once drunk, turns the world up-side-down.

scotch whisky

Scotch whisky is available as either a single malt, distilled in a particular distillery; or as a blend of different single malts, and aged between 12 to 21 years in oak vats. The spelling differs from its American and Canadian cousins: they have an extra 'e'. Irish whisky is spelt the same way but only whisky made in Scotland can be called 'scotch'. Smokier and drier than other whiskeys, Scotch is distilled with peat, giving it its prized, earthy flavour.

tequila

The national spirit of Mexico, tequila originates from the Mexican town of the same name. Cuervo Tequila is the world's largest selling tequila. Like all tequilas, it's made from the native Mexican agave plant which grows in abundance there. Different tequilas pride themselves on the quality of agave used, its oak aging and the flavour characteristics that set them apart from the rest. Tequila is not Mescal, for which it's often mistaken. Mescal has a small pupa worm found commonly in the mescal cactus from which it is made. This is in the bottom of the bottle and to some, is the choicest delicacy of the drink when eaten after a shot.

vermouth

A fortified wine made from herbs, barks and other secret ingerdients. It comes in three common varieties:

Rosso - red in colour and sweet with bitter notes

Blanco - light in colour and fruity in flavour

Dry - slightly darker than blanco in colour, crisper and drier to taste.

vodka

A pure colourless spirit with little or no flavour. However, flavoured vodka is all the rage and my preferred brand, 42 Below vodka from New Zealand, has a great range of flavoured vodkas, including: Manuka Honey, Passionfruit, Kiwi Fruit and Feijoa - as well as its famous, world-beating original pure vodka.

with a whole heap of help from my mates

This book has taken over my life, taken over a year to write, six months of mixing and an eternity to put together. During the journey I have made some great friends. Many who gave their time, ideas and energy for 'nix'. I have to take this page to thank you for everything you've done as I'm only as good as the people who support me.

The buzz, the vibe and the genuine good taste that we have spread all over the world would not happen without such massive amounts of help and dedication from so many special people. I am proud to be part of such a great team and humbled by the faith many of you instil in me. To distil so many passionate people in any order would be impossible.

But I have to start with someone who has sacrificed as much as I to pull this together. Esmeralda, you gave everything for this project and without you and your wise direction, it would never have been such a beautiful book. As my wife, coach, creative force, photographer, designer and chief taste tester - you never seem to run out of energy, love and passion. You're the greatest!... and I love you madly. Sorry for all the things I forgot and the headaches.

Sunil, you are such a wizard wordsmith, bless you and your way with language. Steve MacDonald, Dave Lang, Bodhi Edwards, Adam Gibson, Steve Rodwell, Niko, Will, Tony, Shamlya, Deon and Renata and all the team at MONDO Bartenders for being part of the tireless effort to take the book and show on the road, and keep it the wheels turning. For planning, organising and running around shakin' your asses as it all fell in place, yeah I see you baby! Million ta's to you all.

Special thanks to George and Marina. The media, promoters and honchos: Andrew Batey, Matt Kesby, Melbourne TAFE, COTAH in Brisbane, Weltech in Wellington, Sam at Float, Dona, Gavin and Gail at the team at North Port. Lisa and Verginia Hellier, James, Meghan, Tim, Ashley and the team at AES. Sandy Walker, Kerri-Anne Kennerley and the team at Channel Nine. Ago and Janice, Cristina, Studio Kite, Tracky Dax and all the folk who gave their time, music and ideas to go on camera for the sake of this project. Big big thanks.

To the supporters: with you we are really something! Cristy at Remy and Piper-Heidsieck Champagne. Belinda, John and Brett with Midori and Cuervo. Mary at Grand Marnier, Pedro and Alain at Lipton. Les and Gabriel with Angostura. Ann-Maree and the Ocean Spray team. Craig, Geoff and everyone at 42 Below vodka. Paul, Simon and everyone at Havana Club. Alison and Naomi in the ladies' lounge at Sunbeam. Thanks for your understanding and confidence, you're all great to work with.

To our friends and family who gave their time and energy. Who understand why we have such a little amount of time to spend with them and accept the busy lives we lead. Thanks for being there and helping us through. Bodhi, Gerard, Blair and Sally, Ben and Fahmiya, Christina and PJ, Leonie and Tony, Shyamla, Adam, Stevie, JJ and Dave, love always.

Finally, to the most incredible people in my life, Amalia and Jaime, for all the help you have given me and your wonderful big hearts that just seem to give so continuosly. Thankyou.

One word... beautifulsuperbeffort!

index

Italicized numbers refer to photographs.

recipe index

ingredients index